LIVING YOUR BEST

Third Act

D1521935

HOW TO BE HEALTHY, WEALTHY, AND HAPPY IN YOUR RETIREMENT

DON'T MAKE THE MISTAKES MOST PEOPLE DO

MILAN SCHWARZKOPF

Foreword by Chip Conley

First edition

ISBN 9798884201095 (printed copy)
ISBN 9788011032630 (e-book)

Book writing coach: Jim Connolly
Copyeditor: Sarah Welch, The Wholehearted Editor
Cover design and illustrations:
Mária Fúčelová, Milan Schwarzkopf, Jim Connolly
Photos taken and edited by: Lenka Krobová

Praise for Living Your Best Third Act

"No one addresses the importance and power of fun for your retirement years better than Milan Schwarzkopf! Living Your Best Third Act is a masterpiece that humanizes your retirement plan and creates the ultimate guide to living your most complete and happy twilight years. Read it, apply it, and reap the benefits!"

— Dr. Marshall Goldsmith, Marshall Goldsmith Inc. Dr. Marshall Goldsmith is the Thinkers50 #1 Executive Coach and New York Times bestselling author of *The Earned Life, Triggers,* and *What Got You Here Won't Get You There*

* * *

"The author, Milan Schwarzkopf, has a real handle on the make up of a successful retirement. By addressing his four key areas of living, he has provided a complete picture of living your best life after your career is complete. It's refreshing to know that a book was written by someone who learned in the trenches and not just in academia. You've given people hope and a process for growth and fun in retirement!!"

— Jim Connolly, CEO Chef. CEO and Author of *Cooking Team Building-How You Can Access the Hearts of Your Employees By Way of Their Stomachs*

* * *

"Living Your Best Third Act will motivate and inspire you in becoming the best you can be. Not one of those all sizzle and no steak kind of books. Milan has taken a difficult life subject and humanized it to the benefit of the individual, the spouse and the whole family. A win for all!"

— Eric Lofholm, Master Sales Trainer & President of Eric Lofholm International. Best-selling Author of *The System - The Proven 3-Step Formula Anyone Can Learn to Get More Leads, Book More Appointments, and Make More Sales*.

* * *

"There are many ingredients to a happy retirement and several planning tools that help retirees plan for their own "third act" of life, in new and more meaningful ways. One of the most powerful tools is "Living Your Best Third Act" that you won't find in any other retirement preparatory books. The retirement wisdom and knowledge that you will find in this book will prove to be much more important than how much money you have saved. "Living Your Best Third Act" helps you create an active, satisfying and happy retirement in a way that you don't need a million dollars to retire."

— Dr. Renee Michelle Gordon, Philanthropist, Humanitarian, International Speaker & Author of *Finding Your Love at Last, Five Simple Steps to Attract Your Soulmate Within 90 Days*

* * *

"Living Your Best Third Act is an inspiring book for anyone who wants to create a retirement plan that's not just about being financially comfortable but aimed at helping you to live a vivid and fulfilled life. The book provides the right perspective at the right time, and if you want to build a retirement plan that is both solid as well as inspired, you need to consult this book. Milan Schwarzkopf has done an amazing job in helping you enjoy the best years of your life!"

— Lubna Samara, HigherWill, Founder of HigherWill, Winner of Best Leadership & Spiritual Coaching Co in 2021 of the SME Greater London Awards

* * *

"This is a unique book, tackling a very important but much neglected subject. It's really easy to avoid thinking about one's old age, until it's too late. This guide is very thorough. It deals with all of the objections in a systematic way, and it covers every part of the subject, not just the financial aspects but happiness and health too. Additionally, Milan has generated some truly unique and original models which you won't find anywhere else apart from in this book, so it's a must read for everyone who plans to live until they are old!"

— Chris Croft, Chris Croft Training, Author and Speaker

* * *

"If you have health, you have everything! This author added to everything and gave us three more guiding principles for retirement. Get this book now and reap the benefits of an inspired retirement life!"
— Debbie Saidyfye, Plant-Based Lifestyle Advocate and Author of *Forever Young Eating*

* * *

"Milan Schwarzkopf has nailed it with this book. The timing of his wisdom and the knowledge contained in these pages is an excellent guide to those people seeking to improve the enjoyment and fulfillment of their retirement years. I highly recommend Living Your Best Third Act if you want to create your own best third act!"
— Sidrid Y. Rivera, Sidrid Rivera Enterprises, Author of *I CAN U CAN.*

* * *

"So timely, so perfect! Living Your Best Third Act is the right book, at the right time. As a single Mom of two, there was no time to think about retirement. Now I need to and I could not have a solid retirement plan without consulting with this book. Milan Schwarzkopf has done an amazing job in helping you understand and enjoy the best years of your life!"
— Nicole Grey, Nicole Grey Real Estate, Realtor/Author of *Who's the Baby; Who's the Boyfriend?*

* * *

"As someone approaching my "Third Act," I appreciate how Milan Schwarzkopf has taken a complex topic and broken it down into clear steps. If you want to make the best of your "Third Act," read this book. It will give you a clear game plan for planning, and it will give you clarity and confidence as you approach retirement."
— Tom Ruwitch, Story Power Marketing, Founder and CEO

* * *

"An Inspiring Yet Practical Guide.

This book will nudge you from clueless to confident about your retirement years. Going through this process without the book is a mistake you don't want to make. Milan doesn't just focus on Financial, but also, Health, Social and Lifestyle. Your time and money will be well invested."

— Tommy "Lemonade", CLJ (Chief Lemon Squeezer) of Tommy's Lemonade, Author of *The Lemons God Gives You*

* * *

"Every now and then a book comes along that provides the right perspective at the right time. Living Your Best Third Act is one of those books. You can't build a solid retirement plan without consulting with this book. Milan Schwarzkopf has done an amazing job in helping you enjoy the best years of your life!"

— Aylin Webb, Anxiety & Perfectionism Specialist | Author | Master Coach, CBT & EM DR Therapist | Public Speaker, Psychologist (MSc) | Lecturer (UH) | Podcaster

* * *

"We spend so much of our time dreaming about retirement, but rarely make concrete plans and goals about how we truly want to live during retirement. This often leads to depression and loss of purpose for the newly retired. Milan's book gives you the roadmap you need to plan and prepare for your retirement and truly make your retirement the golden years you deserve! Retirement is so much better if you can use Milan's roadmap to skip the 'figuring it out' stage and get busy living!"

— Rebecca Jensen, CPA, MaxQTC, Inc., 101 West Cascade Way, Suite 102, Spokane, WA 99208

* * *

"Milan Schwarzkopf's book Living Your Best Third Act is rich with wisdom and knowledge to help you create your own best third act. If you are ready to create your best third act, I would definitely get this excellent guide!"

— Judy Wong, Living Out Loud . . .Ain't Over Yet!, Energy Accelerator /Transformation Coach

* * *

"Do you have a retirement plan? If not, it is essential to make one in this age of uncertainty. And if you already have one, are you sure it has been properly thought out? Living Your Best Third Act covers every aspect of planning for retirement, not just the financial matters. Understanding the DNA of a complete and balanced retirement plan is key to enjoying your enjoyment. Milan gets it, and so will you when you read this book. The advice therein is priceless, and the tiny investment will be repaid 100-fold or 1000-fold when the curtain rises on your Third Act."

— Robiyan Easty, Dovetail Publications, Publisher of *The Braids of Kaminari* series and *Ridds for Kids* series

* * *

"Milan Schwarzkopf's understanding that a complete and balanced retirement is much more than the financial aspect of a plan! His book teaches the new fundamentals of retirement that most people desperately want and need. This is a must read for yourself and for your loved ones!"

— Martin Gassner, Liechtenstein Fiduciary Expert for Wealth Structuring and Estate Planning

* * *

"If you're serious about your own third act of life and your retirement, then this is the book for you. Read and apply these principles from this powerful book for your life and well-being!"

— MSc. Jiří Čadek, Head of Wealth Management, MONECO Ltd.

* * *

Disclaimer

The information and statements contained in this book are provided for educational and informational purposes only. The author and publisher shall have neither liability nor responsibility to anyone with respect to any loss or damage caused, or alleged to be caused, directly or indirectly, by the information contained in this book. The ideas, tips, suggestions, techniques, or strategies within it do not guarantee success and are not medical, health care, mental health, financial, tax, investment, or legal advice. The information presented here is not intended to diagnose, treat, heal, cure, or prevent any illness or medical or mental health condition and are not intended to be a substitute for medical advice, diagnosis, or treatment. Never disregard professional medical advice or delay seeking treatment due to information contained herein.

You should take no action solely on the basis of this publication's contents. Any action you take on the basis of the information provided is solely at your own risk and expense. The information presented here is not investment recommendations, investment counseling, accounting services, tax, or legal advice. I am providing services only in the capacity as a coach, not as a licensed medical, health care, mental health, or investment professional. Working with me is not a guarantee of any results. I own all copyrights to the materials presented here unless otherwise noted.

I am a coach, not a psychotherapist or physician, and I am not trained in diagnosing psychological or medical conditions. If any issues come up for you that should be handled by a licensed therapist or physician, I insist you contact the appropriate professional.

I am not responsible for any harm that may arise as a result of the information obtained from this report. All education is provided in good faith and believed to be 100% safe and accurate by the author at the time of authorship.

*I dedicate this book to my sons
Dan and Michal.*

Acknowledgement

I would like to acknowledge my girlfriend, Martina, for her patience and comments; Marisa Murgatroyd, the author of the marketing training I have graduated from; Jim Connolly, my book preparation coach; Lubna Samara, Evi Xyrafa, my colleagues from the marketing training pod; Carolyn Shadrach, my pod coach in the marketing training; Sarah Welch, my editor. And all the great authors from the list of references.

Speaking, Workshops, Online Courses, and Coaching

If you'd like Milan to speak live or virtually at your next event, conference, or meeting, please reach us by visiting our web site, www.thirdactresources.com, or for your convenience, scan the QR code below.

Also, Milan is available for the following:

— Live & Virtual Workshops
— Podcasts
— Radio
— Television
— Breakout Sessions
— Keynote

Once again, visit our web site, www.thirdactresources.com, or for your convenience, scan the QR code below.

www.thirdactresources.com

Contents

Foreword

With innovations in medicine, pharmaceuticals, joint replacements, and holistic treatments, we have gained an extra 30 years of life in the last 70 short years. And, for the first time in history, retirement is as long as 20-30 years (about the same time as studying and gaining your qualification), and if you are healthy, even more. These extra years of life are far from a passive rocking chair existence. What kind of life do you want to create? One that is as deep and meaningful as it is long?

Midlife used to be 45 to 65; it now stretches into a midlife marathon 40 years long, from 35 to 75. Our physical peak may be our twenties; our financial and salary peak may be age 50, but our emotional peak is in midlife and beyond.

We believe the modern elder is as much an intern as they are a mentor because they realize in a world that is changing so quickly, their beginner's mind and catalytic curiosity form a life-affirming elixir, not just for themselves but for everyone around them. A modern elder knows how to intern publicly and mentor privately. A wise modern elder mentor / coach, who has a finely attuned human heart and mind, can offer you the right questions.

In our Modern Elder Academy, we intend to grow a wise community that sees midlife through a new lens. Midlife transitions may be confusing and lonely. We bring with us responsibilities and commitments to family, businesses, careers, and our history. Our decisions start to feel increasingly consequential. We provide a program for people to reframe and repurpose their life experience in their midlife transition and teach them how to be indispensable in the second half of their working life.

Even if they successfully manage their midlife transition, there is another transition in front of them later — retirement. When facing significant change that requires an internal transition to occur, sometimes our fear overrides the impulse to grow. Like with any transition, there will be new Endings (which you have a chance to define and dream of), Messy Middles, and New Beginnings again. And although this transition has been brewing, for decades, it may hit you out of the blue. With this book Milan Schwarzkopf believes it is possible and necessary to prepare for it consciously and shows us the way. He offers you the right questions and provides answers. He shares his knowledge and personal experience. Milan approaches the topic with similar intentions to those we have in the Modern Elder Academy.

Transition to retirement has many differences from the midlife transition. You do not have commitments to business and career anymore (unless you intentionally want to). Your commitments to family and other relationships are qualitatively different. And some other commitments arise or increase in importance (commitment to yourself and your health). And some come back again with new urgency and completely new answers: Purpose. Now it's time to design your purposeful path for every aspect of your Third Act life: personally, physically, psychologically, and spiritually. Milan shows us good approaches in all these pillars.

As for purpose: A recent McKinsey & Co. survey found that 70 percent of people said that their primary sense of purpose is defined by their work. Especially those of you who see your work as a Calling will need intensive inside work to find the path to your new purpose in retirement. It will require you to ask deeper questions about what you value and how you can contribute, aligning your new inner life and your outer life, rewriting your "Success Scripts" that seriously influence how you will define success in your new life, and possibly not being a person of success anymore, but rather a person of value. At MEA, we often say that in midlife we're not just growing old, we're growing whole. By acting in a purposeful manner, good things naturally start to happen. Being "purposeful" will likely lead you to your purpose.

Does it require you stepping out of your comfort zone? Definitely. Miracles happen outside your comfort zone. Is it worth it? Sure.

The challenge of humanity is that living a long time does not guarantee wisdom. Age does not guarantee growth. We must consciously choose that path for ourselves. To do that we need to understand the component parts, nuances, and risks we face in our own transitions. We need a clear anatomy for transitions.

You may live another fifty years; if you knew you may live to the age of 100, what new talent, skill, or interest would you pursue today in order to become a master?

M. L. King: "Be a thermostat, not a thermometer."

From a research point of view, Milan has gone through a lot of available resources on this issue, which have not been summarized anywhere else yet. It is a practical guide for anyone who wants to move in this direction. Taking inspiration from these resources, and adding his practical knowledge and experience gained throughout the decades, Milan shares this book with us and has organized it into a clear and logical system. He provides practical advice, action steps, homework, templates, and exercises. If you follow it, you will not miss anything essential to prepare for your best possible retirement. Milan is dedicated to lifelong learning that helps people live a life that is as deep and meaningful as it is long.

Milan also provides much evidence for why this topic is both important and difficult. On top of the basic four pillars, he provides tools for stress management and routine building and encourages us to understand retirement planning as a project.

Living Your Best Third Act - How to Be Healthy, Wealthy, and Happy in Your Retirement is a roadmap for long-term thinking, ambitious, determined professionals who want to transition well into their retirement, create a retirement action plan, and live healthy, wealthy, happy, and fulfilled in retirement — when the time comes. Then retirement does not happen to you but for you, by your own doing, because you have actually looked at all aspects of how you shift yourself — hence retirement will become a successful transition.

Dear readers, you are in for an eye-opening and transformative book. Sit back and enjoy this journey of discovery.

Chip Conley, Modern Elder Academy's founder, hospitality entrepreneur, and New York Times bestselling author. His book, *Wisdom@Work*, forms the core of MEA's curriculum and is inspired by his experience — as both a mentor and an intern ("mentern") — when he was well into his 50s as Airbnb's Head of Global Hospitality and Strategy.

Preface

For the first time in history, your retirement will be 20-30 years (about the same time as studying and gaining your qualification), and if you are healthy, even more. Although we all prepared for work, nearly nobody is preparing for this longer retirement time. If you are not preparing, it may easily become a tragedy. I want it to be a joy for you, the best part of your life.

I believe everyone deserves a healthy, happy, rich, and fulfilled retirement. Retirement planning is a project. In any project, always begin by defining what exactly a project involves and what is to be achieved. This book should help. This project is yours. You are both the customer and sponsor/investor of the project. You will learn to set your goals and create a plan to achieve them. You will learn to make choices, not adopt the choices of society or others.

The amount of information on this subject is huge, but it has not been available from one source until now. I do not want you to be overwhelmed. I have broken things up into smaller, manageable bites and will lead you on your way. Take a deep breath. We are taking off.

I have worked as a Senior Project Manager on international and global projects for three decades. I made transitions several times: I have lost my job three times during my career (for different reasons) and could not find a new one for several months. It was very demanding not just financially but mainly psychologically. I drew a conclusion: I increased my qualifications (graduating as an MBA), remained within a project manager profession, and became a freelancer (with much higher daily rates) as preparation for the Third Act. When my last project finished many years later, the transition to the Third Act was financially simple, but I must admit it still was psychologically rather complex and took some time. I can imagine how hard it can be for somebody who is unprepared. Later I started to improve my health and learned ways to improve my relationships. And I continue to refine my Third Act life meaning (passing on my knowledge being part of it).

Introduction

Every author hopes for one thing when they dispatch their book out into the world: that readers reap the most benefits possible from their words. I see you as a long-term thinking, ambitious, and determined professional. Probably in your mid to late age, you're worried about your retirement (what I call the Third Act of life). You want to achieve everything possible for you to retire well and have your retirement years be the best time of your life. And you are willing to prepare for it and make that desire a reality.

You'll find the answers to the most obvious questions you've had about retirement. You'll then discover how retirement can become the best part of your life. You will also learn why you should personally care about your retirement, right now. Later on, I'll introduce to you the idea of the Third Act.

You may currently be in the middle of your Second Act — you're still working and fully engaged in making money and completing your career, while also aware that your Third Act will come one day. And you'd like to make the Third Act of your life the best it can possibly be. I will help you realize that preparing for retirement is not just about money. Good relationships matter, too. Crucially, I'll also teach you how to prevent yourself from getting stuck in a mode of Pending Life Purpose (PLP).

Whether you are aware the Third Act of your life is coming up, or you have already started it and want to do it better, you may be asking yourself *What am I missing?* So next we go into more detail about planning your Third Act. You will also learn the dangers of neglecting retirement preparation.

Planning for retirement may be difficult; I will show why. You'll also learn the relationship between beliefs, thinking, feelings, and the results you seek. You will then understand why not many people have a real retirement plan and see the need for vision, discipline, and consistency.

In my view, there are four pillars (plans) to focus on during your Third Act preparation. They are Financial, Health, Social, Lifestyle (aka life meaning, contribution, happiness). After you learn these pillars, accepting full responsibility for the preparation of your Third Act and setting your retirement goals will come naturally.

The most obvious pillar is the Financial plan for retirement. You'll learn the importance of your money mindset, how to get rid of toxic money beliefs, get hints on preparation steps, go through several action steps, and learn a potential financial strategy for watering your wealth tree. Using this system, you will create your retirement financial plan, enabling you to retire financially secure, do almost everything you want, when you want, with whom you want, wherever you want, for as long as you want, and enjoy your wealthy Third Act of life — when the time comes. Your retirement years will be the best time of your life.

The human body has the ability to live 90+ years in good health, so we are playing for at least 8 to 14 more years of a healthy life in retirement, based on the present life expectancy data. Only 10% of life expectancy is influenced by your genes. The rest is determined by your lifestyle.

I like to use a tree metaphor for your health, so I call it planting your "health tree." You will learn the "Health Equation": Understanding the context –> Building the basics –> Planting your health tree –> Watering your health tree. By using these techniques, recommendations, and action steps to keep your health as good as possible, you will become the CEO of your health. Your new lifestyle will ensure you can retire healthy. Imagine being able to do almost anything you want in retirement!

Everyone knows that excessive stress can have a very negative impact on all areas of life and even kill you. I go deeper into how it can affect you, so you can minimize the impact stress has on you.

Social and relationship planning for the Third Act is vital. Social isolation increases the risk of premature death by 30%. You will learn the "Social Plan Equation," consisting of family, friends, and other communities. I will offer you other useful tools, too: how to cope with great anger, the art of living alone, and how to make friends at all levels.

Implementing a retirement social plan will help you enjoy decades of happy life and good relationships before, and in, your Third Act. Imagine doing what you have planned for, when you want to, with whom you want to, when retired.

The last pillar in building your Third Act plan is Lifestyle — mental health care, fulfillment and purpose, and emotional health planning. You will understand the steps to build your emotional health lifestyle plan, possible approaches and techniques, and your attitudes. You will also build your routines. Your new identity, not based on work, will make the decades of your retirement a joy to look forward to and experience fully. Imagine all the personal freedom, leisure, and change of life structure you will gain in retirement. See yourself as a new person, with new desires and possibilities of how to live your new life. You may also add another item (= WHY) to the meaning of your retirement life, so you can make your retirement years the best time of your life.

As you have probably noticed, planning your Third Act is just like planning a project: the project of you. You have an opportunity to take the rest of your life in your hands. You will see why retirement planning is a project, and where you go in this project is the most exciting next step of your life. Project planning can be exciting if you allow it to be, by making the project for you.

Your Third Act may have more structure than the other acts of your life, but you'll learn that proper planning alleviates a lot of stress by knowing where you're going. The Third Act of your life will be the best part of your life because you are thinking about it in advance. You'll set a plan, but with the flexibility of improving upon it during the years to come, it will be ever changing and growing with you.

Whether you are still in the second act of your life, or have crossed over to the Third Act, I know you'll enjoy this book. If at any time you want more information, visit

www.livingyourbestthirdact.com.

Chapter 1: Why Should I Care About Retirement Planning?

> "You must learn from the mistakes of others. You can't possibly live long enough to make them all yourself." Sam Levenson

Are you worried about how you will transition into retirement? What does retiring well look like to you?

Your mission — should you choose to accept it — is to retire well by preparing and implementing a clear, powerful Retirement Action Plan, so you can live a healthy, wealthy, happy, and fulfilled Third Act of life, when the time comes, and have meaning for your fresh start prepared.

Imagine retiring financially secure and healthy, so you can do almost anything you want. And imagine your new identity, not based on work, that will make decades of your retirement a joy to look forward to and experience fully. Also imagine seeing yourself as a new person, with fresh ideas and possibilities of how to live your new life. Finally, imagine doing what you have planned for, when you want, with whom you want, wherever you want, for as long as you want, in your Third Act of life. Your retirement years will be the best time of your life.

Believe me, it's all possible. Others have achieved it, and you can, too. What you think of and believe in will happen. Your outer world reflects your inner world. You own your future. I will assume you want to learn and grow. I want to help you on your way.

Read this chapter to understand:
— Why all people should care about their retirement
— How this book will help you
— What the Third Act is and what it has to do with retirement
— Why retirement isn't just about money
— The scientific research backing up the statements and opinions in this book
Let's dive into this chapter.

Why Is Planning for My Retirement Important?

You probably know other people or relatives who have struggled in retirement (financially, socially, health, lifestyle, or fulfillment), and you don't want the same for you. Security and enjoyment are top priorities, but when looking into the future, you might be afraid of not having enough money, health, purpose, or relationships.

My story: I worked for decades as a project manager, both employee and freelancer, leading large complex international and global IT projects. Responsibility for huge budgets and large numbers of people led to me not sleeping well at night and being over-stressed. In later years, I asked myself: *Why am I doing this? How long can I withstand this? How long do I want to withstand this? Is this job still providing meaning (my WHY), as it did many years before? What will happen if my health deteriorates? Will I be able to live decently from the state pension?*

For many years, I suspected this stressful work and reliance on the state or social security pension would not provide me with enough security for a decent retirement. Also, I knew if I did not prepare in advance, my health, relationships, lifestyle, and fulfillment would deteriorate in retirement, too. For these reasons, I have been purposefully preparing myself for decades for retirement, which I am currently in.

I decided to study what was available on this topic and spent years reading and understanding related books, articles, and other literature, consulted with experts from various professions, watched webinars and trainings of world authors, and did the tasks I have set for myself. I realized all aspects of our lives are interconnected — everything affects everything. When I finished my plan, I had direction and satisfaction in this new way of thinking.

I knew government and politicians would not dictate how

my life is going to be. For a long time, I couldn't imagine how useful it eventually would become. I occasionally only felt the short-term sacrifices. When my last project was stopped, and later when the pandemic hit, I realized I do not have to worry for the rest of my life. I was able to relax when I knew I had implemented a plan. Now I am not worried. I feel secure (even with the pandemic and inflation). I am healthy. I enjoy good relationships. And because I see that many people don't keep retirement in mind and then have various (and not just financial) problems, I wrote this book. I want to share my experience with you.

Why should you personally care about your financials in retirement? You do not have to, if you really trust the "agreement" with the state and politicians will hold true (or your social security or company insurance will provide you enough financial security) and if you believe the future politicians are going to keep the promise that everybody's going to be taken care of, despite how many times they have lied to us. (By the way, that is true in most countries in the world). Looking at yourself in the mirror right now, do you feel like you're prepared to stop working when you will not be able or wanting to work more and not have to worry about paying bills and enjoying your life?

What Will I Learn in This Book?

On a late winter afternoon thirty years ago, two men graduated from the same university. They were much alike. Both had been better-than-average students. Both were personable and filled with ambitious dreams for the future. Fast forward thirty years, and the two men have met again. Since graduation, they've both married, raised families, and gone to work for a great company — the same company, in fact. Two men who seemed to be on identical paths. But their paths diverged.

Now they are both retired. One is financially secure, happy, healthy, enjoying his time, and having good relationships. The other just gets by financially, is having health troubles, is divorced and living alone, has left almost all of his past hobbies, and is always complaining about something. What makes this kind of difference in people's lives? It isn't intelligence (they both are) or talent (they both have it). It isn't that one person wants success and the other doesn't. The difference lies in what each person knows and how s/he makes use of that knowledge. And that is why I'm writing this book. (Adopted from (101)).

I have compiled my 20+ years of knowledge into this book. I basically took the best and left the rest, so you don't have to do all that research. Using my guidance, you can have a roadmap to help you on your own journey. It will be simpler/easier for you to get there than it was for me. You will need somewhat less effort and can avoid dead ends. Much of the information in this book is based on my personal journey, so please customize it to your situation.

Reading the book will help put you on the path to your healthy, wealthy, happy, and fulfilled Third Act of life, and it will show you a holistic roadmap of where you could go by taking actions today. You will still have to work on yourself and set and meet goals, but it's a whole lot better travel time than many years it took me to get to where I'm at now since you can use the advantage of all my knowledge and experience. It is my passion to keep it as simple and straightforward for you as possible.

This is not your typical financial retirement book. The financial plan is not the whole story. I wrote this book because there's no book out there that addresses the whole story about retirement. Other books only address parts of it. Financials are an important part, but you could have all the money put aside and have a plan to take care of yourself till 100 years old, but if you're sick because you didn't take care of your body and assumed your health would always be good; or you have bad or no relationships; or you are depressed because you have no emotional health, fulfillment, or purpose anymore, then you cannot be happy and live the lifestyle you deserve.

My payoff now: I have retired healthy and am enjoying

decades of blissful life in retirement. I retired financially secured and am not worried, and I can do what I want, when I want, with whom I want, wherever I want, for as long as I want.

What Is the Third Act? What Does It Have to Do with Retirement?

Gaining a qualification: 20-30 years	Active life	Third act of life: 20-30 years or more

We have all lived our first act of life, which, like in the first act of a drama, was when we were developing as a human being, starting to know who we were, actually growing up, studying, improving our qualifications, and preparing for our second act of life. In that second act, like in a drama where the character is being developed, we expand our knowledge and expertise, are working, possibly changing our roles, ideally achieving the mastery level, making money to be able to support our family, building a house or renting a flat, buying a car, and preparing resources for retirement.

One day we will retire, and we will not work anymore (unless we want to). We will actually change our life roles. We will live from our savings and investments, pension, social security, or company plans. But there is more to retirement than just the financial part. That's why I use the term "Third Act" of life. It needs a holistic view, including health, relationships, lifestyle, new life meaning (not based on work or profession, which has provided you purpose, community, structure, challenges, accomplishment, and satisfaction), contributions to the world, and happiness.

For the first time in history, the Third Act of life is as long as our first act (20-30 years), and if you are healthy, it will be even more years. Still, nearly nobody is preparing for this Third Act. If you are not preparing, it may easily become a tragedy. I don't want that for you. I want it to be a joy for you, with a long duration.

Imagine you will have, say, 10 to 14 hours a day for yourself. How will you use your time, energy, and resources? Will you be able to improve your health or relationships, which may have deteriorated during your second act?

Why It's Important to Start Now and Not Leave It till Later

You are making money and probably spending the money on your living and your family. You've contributed to the Social Security Administration (SSA) system and maybe a 401(k), or any other one, and you believe the government will take care of you in retirement. But this was never fully true and will be less true in the future.

If you are building your business or career, and also taking care of your family now, you may tend to put off planning for retirement, or the Third Act of life. That's how I used to be. I had been building both my career and my family, and I was taking care of making more money, having bigger projects, and charging higher daily rates. But I gradually started to think *How long can I do this? How long do I want to do this? What will it be like then? One day I won't be able or willing to work that hard, or even harder, anymore, so I'll probably retire.*

I gradually came to the conclusion that relying on only the state pension is not enough, and damaging my family relationships because of too much work is not good. Damaging my health because of high stress, connected with big responsibility, is also not sustainable for a long time.

First of all, in my experience, preparing oneself financially for retirement is a long run. It takes at least 10-15, maybe 20 years. So even now if you are building your business and career, or maybe reaching the top of your career, I believe you should be at least thinking about your retirement, being aware. In my case, when a sudden pay raise or big bonus came, or I got a project with a high daily rate, I realized

I don't have to spend it all. I instead thought about saving and investing it for the years to come.

You may be thinking... *That doesn't sound like fun. It sounds like a lot of work.* The truth is it is not a lot of work. The first step is being aware, disciplined, and being able to set and meet goals for yourself in the long run. The second step is getting some basic information, for instance, by reading this book or attending my course. And the third step is being prepared to seek professional help. Listen to people who have knowledge and are able to condense it in a simplistic but still meaningful way. It also helps to see the bigger picture and the reward for all the preparation work. Visualizing your ideal future now is very helpful for your motivation to set the short-term, intermediate, and long-term goals, which will lead you to an enjoyable Third Act of life.

You may also be thinking... *So I just buy a big house, spend a lot of money, and, when I'm ready to retire, downsize to an apartment and sell my house. Isn't that enough for retirement?* It may or may not be. That depends on many trends. There may be some crises coming. The value of your flat or house can come down. (Do you remember the 2008 "mortgage crisis"?) Your home equity might be less than you think. You may not be able to make enough money from that. You might not be able to sell it for the same money you bought it for. And you cannot assume the return from your real estate is always bigger than from other investments. You can't predict what the economic conditions (inflation, home prices, etc.) will be when you retire. Hope for the best and plan for the worst. What if your home equity was half of what you expected at retirement? Could you successfully navigate that challenge? What can you do now just in case?

You cannot plan for all of that in advance. The only reasonable thing you can do is diversify your investments, not putting all your eggs in one basket and not relying on one asset only. And, in my view, because this portfolio planning is pretty complicated, and not many of us are able to do it for ourselves, I would recommend hiring an independent professional advisor or portfolio manager. But the first step is to understand the importance of this topic.

I Don't Know What I'll Do in Retirement and Don't Want to Bother Myself, So I'll Just Wait until I Get There, Right?

You don't have to. My friend and classmate John, a funny and smart man, former investment banker, mountaineer, rafter, and kayaker, whom I used to travel with, did not plan for his retirement. He is now boring, ill, not very well financially, and living alone. He surely was successful in the first two acts, i.e., both during his studies and his career; however, he did not plan for his Third Act, as is the case with most people. Each act has a distinct purpose. The Third Act is most important, as it binds everything together, can bring meaning (not based on work) to all that you did, and it may last 20-30+ years.

Lately, when my coach Jim asks people about their retirement, they all say the same thing: "Well, for the first 10 years we'll probably travel a lot. I don't know what we're going to do after that." It doesn't sound like a real plan, does it?

Many people think they will just focus on their hobbies that they never had time for. Can that be their retirement? Yes, it can. Many people do so, but are you sure you don't need anything else? And, if you didn't have enough hobbies before, or if you didn't have enough time for your hobbies, are you sure your new or refreshed hobbies are able to both fill 10 hours a day of your time and provide you complete life meaning for 20 or 30 years?

A well-known chef in the Bay area was all about food, and when he retired, it took him eight years to let go off his identity as a chef. Now he spends a lot of his time painting. He's always loved painting, and painting is now his passion. It's his creative outlet, and he has very complete life that he never knew he would enjoy. But it took him so long, and he said, "I wish I had not wasted eight years holding on to what I had done all my life, so I could devote my life to art, to where it is now because I could never see myself doing anything but cooking. Now I see so much more." (154)

This reminds me of a story from my own life. One day, when my last project was done, I realized I just didn't want to be a project manager anymore, and, thanks to my preparation, I was able to completely change my lifestyle, which I managed within two or three months. By planning, you're able to transition faster and enjoy the active Third Act more, instead of it being an echo of your second act (your work life).

Retirement Isn't Just about Money

Most people assume retirement is only about money. But even if they manage to save enough money, if they are not healthy, have bad or nonexistent relationships, and are not clear on their new life mission and purpose, they will struggle.

During the second act, job functions and titles shape how people are perceived by themselves and others. Career identities hide our true selves. For people who define themselves primarily through their jobs, losing work or retiring is a serious problem. For people who learn how to create a well-balanced life aside from their job, retirement is not such a big problem. Sooner rather than later, you should positively redefine who you are.

It is common but dangerous to look for meaning in work because it is easy to get carried away. It's an easy pitfall, though, because there often is real meaning in work, and it can often be the *only* "meaning" of life. (67)

In the end, what will be important is your relationships with your children, how you will have treated your parents, how many good friends you have made in your life, and who will want to spend time with you. All your power, money, contacts, insurance, or vacations will be useless if you're a jerk that no one wants to be with any longer than necessary. (67)

Close relationships protect people from life dissatisfaction, help delay mental and physical decline, and bring a long and happy life more reliably than social status, IQ, financial situation, or even genes. (100) Many years ago, life could be characterized as a survival economy. Now there isn't such need to devote so much to economics at the expense of self and loved ones. Each of us needs to keep a careful eye on that for ourselves. (67)

Some people say, you know my parents, they didn't really prepare. They were good financially, so they were "fine." But they were kind of miserable, and their bodies and minds and relationships were falling apart.

Also, many people have idealistic views of their future retirement. They think they have enough hobbies they don't have enough time for now, and their hope is once they have stopped working (and assuming they will have enough resources), they will simply devote their time to hobbies, possibly to some traveling, grandchildren, play golf, and that's it. They think they don't have to prepare. They don't see the hours, weeks, months, years of free time, the impact on health and relationships, the need to align with their spouse, the need for complete lifestyle redefinition, and for most people, the need for contribution, to reach real happiness.

If they do not see it in time, they may spend their time visiting doctors, or worse, making the couch, the fridge, and the TV their three best friends.

Most people are only focused on money and don't look at the rest of their life in a holistic way. My friend's family was planning to travel for the next 10 years. They are now searching for the perfect place to be in retirement. They want to spend time as grandparents, so they can't travel too far, and they can't find their ideal place close to family, so they seem already in a rut, and they haven't even gone fully into retirement.

My method focuses more on the internal part of retirement, whereas most methods are totally external, meaning "I have money, and that's all I need to be concerned with." But money itself cannot make you happy. I have some details later on about research on how much money is actually needed for you to survive and if money contributes to happiness. Sooner or later, you will discover you need more from life. You need internal satisfaction. You need life meaning. Many people discover they need to give back what they have learned or help others. Actually, I am writing this book partially for this motivation, too.

This book is offering an internal solution to what people perceive as an external problem. The problem with most retirement books is they are all about external solutions because they view it as an external problem. The Third Act is an internal problem. Once you have internal strength, you will be able to react well to any future external problems that may arise. My work helps people project themselves into the future. They can design whatever life they want; it doesn't have to be the same way it's always been.

Many people are stuck in Pending Life Purpose (PLP). They're not working (they have left their second act), and they're not retired (are not in their Third Act fully). They are in the middle. My friend recently shared this with me: He is working with a client who needs to learn his purpose now. He's in the second act of his life, and he doesn't understand his purpose, which is affecting his work. He's an independent person and works as a chef for a restaurant group. He's very good at what he does, but the company keeps moving him from one city to the next. It takes away a lot of his freedom. He didn't see the urgency of doing something about it until my friend pointed it out. Then he realized how important it is to him.

What's interesting about the whole idea of finding purpose is sometimes you are able to choose purpose, and sometimes purpose will choose you because of who you are and what you're made of. This man's purpose is not being brought out. Many people know there's a purpose for their higher self, but they're afraid. Their fear prevents them from being all they can be, even though they know they need to change. Some don't want to figure it out. They may think

I've done enough work for other people. I don't want to think about what I'm supposed to do again. So they just continue doing what they are used to in the second act, or even in the Third Act.

According to polls done:
— 27% of retirees have struggled with the transition from work to retirement.
— 61% of retirees said they wish they had done a better job planning for the financial aspects of retirement.
— 54% wish they had done a better job planning for the non-financial aspects.
— 93% say, "It's important to feel useful in retirement."
— When it comes to what pre-retirees have thought a great deal about with respect to their retirement planning, most commonly folks are concerned with "how to save enough to last through retirement" — and at that, only 37% have given this a "great deal of thought."
— 77% of those who are planning to retire wish "there were more resources available to help them plan for an ideal retirement beyond just their finances." (34, 86)

Are The Statements and Opinions in This Book Based on Science and Research?

Senator Daniel Patrick Moynihan: "You are entitled to your opinion. But you are not entitled to your own facts."

Although preparation for retirement is important, it is not taught in schools or systematically lectured, nor have I found comprehensive literature on it. I searched for answers to many questions I had but found only fractions of them.

The statements and opinions are based both on new scientific knowledge (see the list of over 160 references) and my experience. My opinion was the inspiration for this book, and the more research I did, the more I realized the importance of getting this information out to everyone. I've seen firsthand how critical all these elements are in my own life.

According to the Global AgeWatch Index, in 2023 one in every five Americans will be over 65. In 2050, one in five in the world (almost 2 billion people) will be over 60 years old. (17) Think about how you prepare yourself.

Panthera LIFE has shown these retirement observations (34):

Attributes of those who have **NOT** retired well:	Attributes of those who **HAVE** retired well:
— Lack of challenges	— Bucket list
— No considered PLAN	— Purpose-driven activities
— Fear of spending money	— Community engagement
— No hobbies (or not enough)	— Well planned
— Boredom	— Routines
— No active social network	— New identity
— Intellectual decline	— Positive family relationships
— Loss of identity	— Physical activity
— Marital strain	— Work (at least part time)

The National Academy of Sciences found happiness increases at about 52 years. And happiness is still increasing up to age 85. Also, **people who can be positively tuned live longer, on average by about 7.5 years**. (Other surveys suggest anything between 6 and 10 years, according to Shirzad Chamine (20) and Martin Seligman.)

In this book, I summarize knowledge from various sources and many years of my experience. I teach you what has worked for me. Your path may be different. Do not hesitate to customize it for yourself. Be open, try it for yourself, and select what is most relevant for you.

Can You Guarantee Results?

No. I assume you want to learn and grow, and I will help you. I believe everyone deserves a healthy, happy, rich, and fulfilled Third Act of life. But you own your future. You must recognize the seriousness and importance of this topic. You must take action to make your retirement as great as possible. You need a clear action plan to keep you focused on what to do and stick to it for a long time. You must be ready to visualize ideals about life in retirement, be willing to significantly change your thinking (transformation), and have long-term discipline to achieve your goals.

Petr Ludwig: "Discipline is your overall ability to take specific actions that lead to the fulfilment of your personal vision."

If you don't plan, and if you don't meet your goals, you may easily end up in PLP status and may not complete your transition to your Third Act of life. You will not be as happy as you could be. This book is a guideline. I can show you how to get up to the mountain. I can draw a map. I can even hold your hand to the top of the mountain, but you must customize it all to your situation and take the steps along with me.

You have unlimited potential inside you. The fact that you're reading this right now means that you're willing to take action to make your Third Act as great as possible. You've already taken the first step.

Jim Rohn: "Discipline is the bridge between goals and accomplishment."

Benjamin Hardy: "Success isn't that difficult; it merely involves taking twenty steps in a singular direction. Most people take one step in twenty directions."

☐ Your homework: Acknowledge your potential challenges and obstacles in Third Act preparation so you can address them. List all the reasons that may be holding you back from starting. Write for at least two minutes.

Potential challenges/obstacles holding me back:

_____

_____

_____

_____

_____

_____

_____

_____

_____

Chapter 2: Why Should You Care about Planning for Your "Third Act"?

> "What we fear of doing most is usually what we most need to do." Ralph Waldo Emerson
>
> "Don't judge each day by the harvest you reap, but by the seeds you plant." Robert Louis Stevenson, Scottish Author

For the first time in history, the period for which we live our retirement is 20-30 years, but most people are not preparing, or are preparing the wrong way. But retirement does not have to be a bad, surprising experience if you avoid common obstacles, get rid of retirement myths, see the dangers of neglecting retirement preparation, and decide repeatedly for many years whether to do what is easy or what is needed.

Are You Getting Older or Growing Older?

In this chapter you will find:
— Why you need to know more about Third Act planning, even if you may already have a retirement plan or are putting money away
— How having a more complete plan will impact your life
— What's different about your retirement generation
— How you can protect yourself from cultural challenges
— How Third Act planning can save you from future challenges
— The dangers of neglecting retirement preparation
— What does science say about happiness, and how does it relate to age

Let's get into this chapter.

Why You Need to Know More about Third Act Planning, Even if You May Already Have a Retirement Plan or Are Putting Money Away

Classical financial advice involves a narrower focus on accumulating and investing money, with no regard for health, happiness, or enjoyment of retirement.

Many people anticipate changes in business, but the same doesn't often apply with the "Third Act." Even though we know our lives are more important than business, most of us, even the most successful ones, are not preparing for retirement, or are preparing a wrong way. The good news is it's possible to retire healthy, financially secure, live as a rentier (living on income from your savings and investments), and enjoy decades of happy life and good relationships. Anyone with the desire can achieve this (with a good degree of probability). I originally did not believe it to be possible but achieved it. Today, I live the satisfied and happy life of a rentier.

Retirement does not have to be a bad, surprising experience. Relying on the state or social security pension only will not provide you with enough funds for a decent retirement (due to demographic trends, climate crisis, debt crisis, etc.). Financially, look beyond just the pension statement.

A couple I know are financially well off, unless something dramatic happens. Their biggest challenge is they don't know where they want to call home anymore. They are on a wild search. They are looking outside of themselves for the perfect place to live, and this is what their retirement has been all about, as opposed to looking from within and figuring out what their purpose is. They live a very structured religious life and are following that to give them purpose. But it's not their purpose. It's the religious structure's purpose. It forces them to look outside of themselves and not within. If they spent more time on their inner journey (looking for their purpose), they wouldn't have to spend all this time and money.

You will find tools, both for where to live in your Third Act and for your inner journey, later on in this book.

My friend's family used to only do what everybody else did, and they hated where they lived. They then looked at all the different aspects of their personalities, what their purpose in life is, and what they expect to be doing for the next 20 or 30 years, and they found a place to live where they have never been before (except for visiting once). They love that it matches all their criteria. They do many things they never did before and are happy.

Such a conscious decision can be made during your second act and re-evaluated for your Third Act, as your selection criteria may change. It all depends on the person or the couple, and you should be having that conversation. You have choices, and that's what's so beautiful about it.

How Having a More Complete Plan Will Impact Your Life

No one plans to be poor, fat, and unhappy; that only happens to people who don't have a plan. Retirement planning is far more than just the finances. You should prepare for a wealthy, healthy, social, fulfilled, and happy retirement. And you do not have to do it alone.

Benjamin Franklin: "Many men die at twenty-five and aren't buried until they are seventy-five."

My friend's brother is not willing to create any plan and has been acting old since his forties. He's merely surviving (financially, socially), without energy or self-esteem, and is missing all of life's opportunities. And his son is copying the same pattern.

Be aware of the importance of this topic. And be curious. Curiosity will keep you young beyond your years. Read. Study. Prepare a strategy and do your homework. Have discipline.

Brian Tracy: "Continuous learning is the minimum requirement for success in any field."

My friend's neighbor is thirty years but acting old. His attitude right now is what could be described as someone who's lived a life of regret and unhappiness. He sees his life ahead of him, and he doesn't see the opportunity. All he sees is negativity. This mindset is aging him. He wants to do things about his health, such as working out at the gym and eating differently but says it's "out of his element." He hasn't been able to change his attitude to a positive one, to see what is possible. That would retain his youth.

What people miss in retirement:
—   Sense of identity & purpose
—   A reason to get up in the morning
—   Social connections
—   Mental and physical stimulus
—   A sense of accomplishment and satisfaction
—   Structure & routine
—   Having a salary (34)

What's holding you back?

What you resist persists.

Procrastination can be the most expensive way.

Petr Ludwig: "The time we spend on Earth is both limited and finite. In light of these facts, time is the most valuable commodity you have in life. It's not money; unlike time, you can borrow it, save, or earn more. You can't do that with time. Every single second you waste is gone forever." (73)

If you are aware of the problems in time, you can often pretty easily and cheaply tackle them. If you procrastinate, the problem will not go away. It will only grow. And the later solution will be much more expensive both financially and mentally, or the solution may not be possible at all.
(You will have missed the opportunity window.)

Andy Storch: "Often, when people set big goals, they get overwhelmed with everything they need to do and then start procrastinating. One of the biggest and best methods for beating procrastination is to start taking action right away." (75)

Everyone loves a happy ending, especially in the story of their own life. Start writing that ending today. And if you are wondering how some people create beautiful and rich Third Acts of life, then the first possible answer is simple. Just start working on it. Either it works... or it doesn't. But if you don't start, you won't know.

What's Different about Your Retirement Generation

Job functions and titles shape how people are perceived by themselves and others. Career identities hide our true selves. For people who define themselves primarily through their jobs, to lose work or retire is a serious problem. So before or soon after retirement, you should positively redefine who you are.

The Top Five Regrets of the Dying (according to Australian palliative carer Bronnie Ware. No. 1 and 5 are my picks):

1. **I wish I'd had the courage to live a life true to my self, not the life others expected of me.**
2. I wish I hadn't worked so hard.
3. I wish I'd had the courage to express my feelings.
4. I wish I had stayed in touch with my friends.
5. **I wish that I had let myself be happier.** (136)

Common obstacles (to be avoided) in retirement planning are:
— Substantial neglect of essential aspects of life (in favor of other aspects, e.g. work).
— Poking your head into the sand (retirement is that far), no planning.
— Reluctance or inability to take responsibility for one's life.
— Prioritization of short-term goals.
— Thinking only of others (children, etc.) and not of oneself.
— Financial, medical, mental ignorance (and unwillingness to get advice or help).
— Unclear life strategy and goals.
— Little discipline in fulfilling one's goals.

As Olivia S. Mitchell says: "Growing awareness of real-world shocks, including market downturns, health surprises, and labor market shifts, calls into question whether global retirement systems will be able to sustain current and future retirees. The long-term scarring effects of these shocks will force us to save more, work longer, and probably expect less." (40)

We all can see stories of what is going to be different about this retirement generation: real-world shocks, like impacts of climatic change (heat waves, droughts, floods) or the war in Ukraine, which is changing the economy (energy prices, inflation). Hence, retirement budgets of many people who did not plan and were poking their heads into the sand are on the edge. Some of these trends could have been predicted, some not. Some exaggerated the predictable trends; some are creating new circumstances for your Third Act of life. Some have multiple impacts, like not enough water for drinking, agriculture, or transportation on the rivers, including coal for power plants (Germany) or cooling of nuclear power plants (e.g. in France). It is important to build reserves for these types of situations or for possible health deterioration.

The impact of the COVID-19 pandemic on the decision to retire: some people "reassess[ed] priorities and lifestyle." Many decided to retire early or take redundancy. The desire for a potentially calmer pace of life increased too, with people wanting to spend less time in crowded cities and more time in rural areas. (34)

Approximately one in three Americans planning to retire said the pandemic altered their retirement timing, as of March 2021. 14 million people had stopped contributing to their retirement accounts. Most Americans (70%) have seen the pandemic as a financial wake-up call, saying it "caused them to pay more attention to their long-term finances." (86)

Albert Einstein taught at Princeton University. His class of advanced physics students was taking an exam. On the way to his office, his assistant, who was carrying the prepared answers, asked: "Dr. Einstein, weren't those the same questions you asked the class last year?" Dr. Einstein replied, "Yes, they were." The assistant, in spite of all respect for perhaps the greatest physicist of the 20th century, asked again, "Excuse me for asking, Dr. Einstein, but how could you ask the same questions to the same class two years in a row?" Einstein simply replied, "The answers have changed."

How Can You Protect Yourself from These New Cultural Challenges?

Retirement is a predictable situation, making planning easier, but it needs to be prioritized.

Get rid of the most common retirement myths:
— Before you retire, you need to have at least XXXXX in your pension.
— You can't retire before the state pension age.
— I have lots to do. I will be busy.
— I will have to reduce my spending in retirement.
— Retirement means the end of work.
— People work in retirement because they need the money. (34)

What are you afraid of in connection with aging? Many of these are legitimate concerns, but few realize that they are influenced by the culture in which you are aging. Aging is hampered by various prejudices (-isms, discriminations), for instance: ageism. Don't be swayed by them. **Aging is life, not a problem that needs to be cured.** All prejudices against the elders are the problem of others, not yours. Whether you perceive yourself as having entered old age will depend upon your attitude more than anything else. Have your sense of purpose. Don't let it be ruined by prejudices, culture, or by other people. (1)

Do not go with the masses. Think of what you really want out of retirement, what would make you happy, and not what others do or what others want from you. This is not easy at all in Western consumer society. Try not to be fully influenced by the way your parents acted or what your partner thinks. It is your life, and it will be your life in retirement. Take responsibility for yourself. (31)

Do not allow any prejudices or other people to shape your expectations and beliefs of the "right" time to retire. Retirement is coming. Keep that in mind and get ready for it.

Ashton Applewhite: "I hope I get old before I die."

Robin Sharma: "The place where your greatest discomfort lies is also the spot where your largest opportunity lives."

The optimal thing is to **have a clear strategy and goals, focus on effort, process, and discipline, and reward yourself with little things for partial steps (and even for embarking on the journey at all), and be satisfied with it**. Wisely consider the balance between momentary satisfaction and fulfilment of long-term goals. You can also take a guide (like this book, a course, or a coach). Or just tell someone your goals. They will become more binding to your subconscious.

You probably know the Aesop tale "The Ant and The Grasshopper." (132) The moral of the story is: "Make hay while the sun shines." One must make the best use of the present situation, instead of suffering later. We need to plan for the future and start working today to reap the benefits tomorrow.

"Before you retire, you need to have at least XXXXX in your pension." That's just a story told by insurance agents. They are always asking "What's your lifestyle like now?" and "When you retire, to duplicate your lifestyle the way it is right now how much money would that mean you have to have?" But it's a myth. The truth is you'll have a completely different lifestyle and criteria then. Insurance agents do not look at the holistic part of your life. That's really poor planning. It gives you a false sense of security.

How Can Third Act Planning Save Me from Some of These Future Challenges?

Retirement is one of life's situations where we can look at where we have been, think about where we are going, and think about what really matters to us. Of course, we do not have to wait for such life situation to occur. We can think about our lives and what we want from them at any time. You are never too old or too young to look at the design of your life. And it's never too late or too early to create the life you want! Clarify your long-term strategy. To do this, we need to know who we are and what our values and priorities are.

Retirement is a bigger change than you think, so planning is important. And it's about long-term planning. To measure our expectations about the potential long-term benefits of any activity when carrying out normal short-term activities (whether at home or at work), questions can help. In this case, *How does this activity help me achieve my goal of preparing for a successful retirement?*

Retirement is not an acute problem. You will have to decide repeatedly for many years whether **to do what is easy or what is needed (what life demands of you)**. It will often be a short-term sacrifice and a conscious departure from the comfort zone in favor of long-term goals. We will have to say a strong "No!" to a lot of things.

No matter what stage of your career you are at, it is good to think about leaving one day. Time is running fast.

How many times have you thought, *How nice would it be to have enough money to never have to work again?* We think of everything we won't have to do: We won't have to get up early, go to work, meet deadlines, or be stressed. But it is difficult to find fulfilment in what we will not do. **We can find fulfilment and meaning only in what we will do.** (2)

When I was young, I believed I could create a successful startup. I had an idea and started the company, providing both the funds and lots of effort. We created the product, but it never really hit the market. I built another startup, again with no success. One day, I realized I have no more time for such experiments. Instead, I started to plan for my Third Act.

In a few years, you will want to have started today. Decide that you accept full responsibility for your preparation for retirement. Don't complain about anyone or anything. Once you say "I am responsible," you cannot blame others.

More than crisis, we are plagued by lack of vision. And here it is: If you do not live your vision, you risk living someone else's vision. Take control of your future... because if you don't, someone else will. It may be your parents, children, government, politicians, or boss. There is always somebody who believes they know best what you should do with your time, money, and effort.

Freedom is not always as easy as it appears. Saul Alinsky: "The greatest enemy of individual freedom is the individual himself."

I had a classmate who became the director of a big logistics company, successfully meeting expectations of the stakeholders. He was making much more money than anyone from our class. His family missed him. Later, he got divorced. When the crisis came, he lost his life meaning and direction.

You should always consider your own vision and future against the "obligation" of trying to please other people and the associated cost.

Ask yourself regularly: *Where am I going? What do I want? Why? What is the real meaning?* Otherwise, the day will come when you regret your path. Your conscience will be heard.

The Dangers of Neglecting Retirement Preparation

As recent research shows, the primary concerns for retirees in order were:

— running out of money
— maintaining their standard of living
— ongoing/longevity of health in retirement
— long-term care costs
— funding travel overseas
— replacing the social aspects of work
— the need to clear outstanding debt (35)

According to Bloomberg, the world's retirees risk running out of money a decade before death. Global retirement shortfall could top $400 trillion by 2050. (102) From the U.S. to Europe, Australia to Japan, retirement account balances aren't increasing fast enough to cover rising life expectancy. The result could be workers outliving their savings by as much as a decade or more. Unless more is done, older people will either need to get by on less or postpone retirement. You either spend less or you make more. The retirement savings gap is about 10 years for men in the U.K., Australia, Canada, and the Netherlands. Longer-living women in those countries face an extra two to three years of financial uncertainty. Across the world, governments and employers have pushed more responsibility for retirement onto individuals, by shifting from traditional pensions to defined contribution plans, mostly known as 401(k) plans in the U.S.

Besides the fact retirement itself can be a hard, stressful, difficult step, we also have a demographic crisis: the aging of the massive boomer generation. Americans aged 65 and older have grown from 35 million in 2000 to 86 million in 2050. (86) The ratio of the number of pensioners to the productive population will increase by tens of percent in the productive population will increase by tens of percent in the EU by 2050 (in Spain and Slovakia even by 100%). (137) And there is more than just a demographic crisis.

The climate crisis will make clean water and air more expensive (either directly financially or indirectly in limiting one's own comfort, luxury, and possibilities, e.g. travel). This is amplified by the debt crisis — even before the pandemic, many countries were on the path to unsustainable public finances due to the absence of pension reform. The pandemic has only made state budget debts worse. Differences between people will grow greatly. The supposed "certainties" from the government may mostly disappear.

So think about how you will prepare yourself. As a man sows, so shall he reap. I want to help you with that. My mission is to pass on my knowledge, so I developed this book and my course. I have spent a lot of time studying literature, buying books and trainings from world authors, and practically preparing for my own retirement. I still don't have all the answers, but I do provide you the foundations, principles, and guidance to develop your strategy. What you'll find in this book goes way beyond what can be found in any single book elsewhere.

Retirement planning is specific in its longevity. But it is your choice. You can live now and suffer later. You can select the pain of discipline or the pain of regret.

If you do not wish to suffer in the Third Act, it is necessary now to **decide and take disciplined, purposeful action in the direction of your goals**. It will be your life in retirement.

Consider the balance between momentary satisfaction and fulfilment of long-term goals. And be sure to imagine the future in the best possible colors.

When I made the decision to set aside a certain amount of money, my lifestyle did not change that much. I have both saved reasonable amounts regularly and used periods of high-daily-rates projects to put the money aside and invest for long-term, not frivolously spending money on useless items. I know many freelance project managers who live a feast and famine life. This was never my choice.

There are many people who spend with no long-term outlook, be it big purchases, like getting a new car every year, or "small" day to day purchases, like eating out every night. Changing such habits will allow you to put money away. At first, it may seem like a bother, but then you'll realize it's not a big deal with a little bit of planning.

My friend Jim decided to go to restaurants with purpose instead of habitually. He started to plan his meals better and discovered he can make meals for the week for the price of one restaurant visit. This is more nutritious than the restaurant food and a whole lot cheaper. This decision probably saved him thousands of dollars every month, which could easily be put aside for a rainy day. By doing this, and by investing the saved money wisely, he is expanding his well-being into the future.

If you're not disciplined, you're going to suffer later. Often, it is enough to stop wasting money on silly things. Changing bad habits isn't suffering; it's a conscious change. And it can be done without really hurting your lifestyle (and even improving your health). Consider if it's truly a need vs. a want/habit. Create new habits that support what you desire.

Do you love yourself? If yes, you do not have to prove to yourself and others that you're worthy or can afford all this spending.

There was a TV producer and director who spent almost all his money when he was in his second act of life. He thought it was good for business. On a regular basis, he would invite people to dinner because he wanted them to work with him on future projects and keep in touch. His sister, who was a teacher for her whole life, had a completely different lifestyle. She rarely took people out to dinner, maybe only for her birthday. She put her money away. Then in their Third Act of life, there were times when he had to go to her to borrow money. He ended up not living very long in his Third Act for various reasons. He lacked money, but he also couldn't maintain the lifestyle he was used to.

Besides meeting basic needs, you always have an alternative. Most choices are habitual. You think you need to spend money on things that you really don't need, instead of thinking about where you could use that money wisely. You can break a habit by creating a new habit. What is it that you really desire?

You are where you are today because you chose so. You thought you couldn't do otherwise. But you always have a choice. Now and in the future.

Some people may be saying, "I don't want to be a millionaire." They may mix wealth with morality, thinking good morals means to hate the idea of accumulating wealth. But here's another view from Gaur Gopal Das, author of *The Way of the Monk*: "As long as people of weak character hold all the resources, society remains in chaos. This is because the resources are used for destructive, self-aggrandizing, and selfish purposes. However, if the resources are transferred to the virtuous, they are used constructively for social contribution and as a medium to serve others."

The meaning of money is how you apply it. If you secretly hate money or "don't want to be rich," your subconscious will work to keep it away from you. But if you can see money as a potential source of good, this is the way forward, both for you and others.

Social Security/ Pension Will Take Care of Me. Why Should I Plan More?

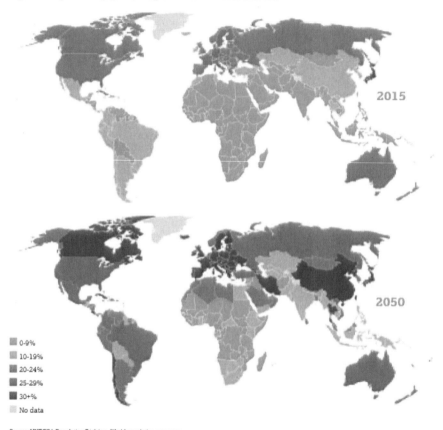

Figure 3: Proportion of population aged 60 or over in 2015 and 2050

2015

2050

- 0-9%
- 10-19%
- 20-24%
- 25-29%
- 30+%
- No data

Source: UNDESA Population Division, *World population prospects: the 2015 revision*, DVD Edition, 2015

What is the biggest myth about retirement? According to a recent retirement survey, almost half of respondents (45%) said the biggest myth was "You don't need to plan your finances in advance," closely followed by "The government will look after you" (30%). Fifteen percent cited "Your pension will always be enough to live on." When asked what they would do differently if they were retiring next year, 30% said they would save more earlier on in their life. (78)

In 2023, one of every five Americans will be over 65. In 2050, one in five in the world (almost 2 billion people) will be over 60 years old. (155) To the see the full world map with color legend go to **www.livingyourbestthirdact.com**.

Oldest age at which 50% of babies born in 2007 are predicted to still be alive.

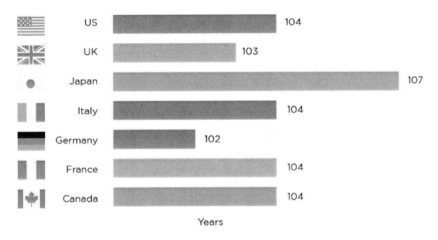

Country	Years
US	104
UK	103
Japan	107
Italy	104
Germany	102
France	104
Canada	104

Years

Source: Human Mortality Database, University of California, Berkeley (USA) and Max Planck Institute for Demographic Research (Germany). Available at www.mortality.org

The pension and Social Security system have long been heading to huge deficits. It is not clear where we will take money for pensions or how we will provide people with enough healthcare or enough money for basic needs, such as food, water, electricity, and rent. Growing awareness of real-world shocks, including market downturns, demographic trends, social, economic, populist, and political trends now significantly strengthened by pandemic effects, energy crises, impact of the war in Ukraine, health surprises, and labor market shifts, calls into question whether global retirement systems will be able to sustain current and future retirees.

The long-term scarring effects of these shocks will force us to save more, work longer, and probably expect less. (17)

There is going to be a shortage of care facilities and care nurses. Many are already finding that right now and we haven't even hit our peak yet. You need to have a plan of what you're going to do if you're overweight, have high blood pressure, have diabetes, etc. Your possibilities of extra care go up tremendously, so you need to take care of those health problems before you're in the Third Act. Otherwise, the worst-case scenario is it will put you in a situation where your care is going to overburden you financially to the point where you cannot afford to be sick.

You want to be clear of your ideal lifestyle now and how to continue that lifestyle. Consider who you'll be when you're in that age group and where you may need extra physical care. You may be in other situations that you didn't think of when you were younger, e.g. needing someone to assist you if your significant other, who you were dependent on your whole life, disappears. Don't only prepare financially. Think of improving your health, your relationships, and your mental health now. Do not stay in the Pending Life Purpose. It doesn't matter how much insurance you have; the reality is going to cost you in so many ways. Social security/pension will not fully take care of you.

Viktor E. Frankl: "The one thing you can't take away from me is the way I choose to respond to what you do to me. The last of one's freedoms is to choose one's attitude in any given circumstance."

Transition to Retirement Will Be Very Pleasant. I Will Not Have to Work, Deal With My Boss, Wake Up Early, or Have Any Stress. I Will Have Time for My Hobbies, Travel, Garden, and Children. Why Should I Worry at All Now?

The first week, month, or six months will be good. This is called the "retirement honeymoon." But then retirement can be a hard, stressful, difficult step and completely different than you thought.

The transition into retirement is one of the major disruptors in life, often with unforeseen problems. The respected Holmes and Rahe stress scale determined that retirement is #10 out of the top 43 stressors in life.   (104)

And remember, 20-30 years or more of your happiness in the Third Act of life is at stake. (2) It's easy to talk about it or look forward to it, but leaving work hurts, especially if you had a job as your best friend and a substantial part of your identity, and if work has brought you benefits such as leadership, relationships, contributions, meaning, and happiness. (31) If work became the basis of your identity, it provided you with structure and routine. But your happiness will not care how hard you have worked in your career.

Research has confirmed that lack of fulfillment together with feelings of irrelevance and loss of identity are common among retirees. It's a direct result of drifting into retirement without a non-financial plan that would address the mental, physical, social, and spiritual side of retirement. (104)

According to literature, the need to face retirement, or the end of a career, is a critical self-learning experience for leaders and one of the tools for survival in the VUCA world (that is, Volatile, Uncertain, Complex, and Ambiguous). (10) Even the world's top leaders can't handle the transition well.

Retirees, when compared to younger Americans, are far more likely to say that "having a sense of purpose" in life is necessary to achieve optimal well-being (69% vs. 55%). It's become clear that all four pillars —health, family, purpose, and finances — are essential to achieving optimal well-being in retirement. (86)

The first few months of retirement can be difficult, particularly for people who didn't have an excellent work/life balance in their careers. Research shows this transition can affect one in five individuals seriously, leaving them in a state of mild or severe depression. (31)

Nobody really talks about planning for their retirement, but you should be putting some of that second act time into planning for the Third Act, just like you did for your career. If you had a successful career, think about what it took to have that. Now is the time to take that same understanding of planning, so you can apply that to your Third Act of life.

In the past, people did not have as many challenges as we do now with all the uncertainties in many areas and also because they didn't live as long. It was not much to plan for. Isn't growing older a beautiful gift we have now?

You may consider taking my course as well. This book is more about awareness. The course and my coaching will put you into action and hold you accountable to preparing your plan and getting it done.

Veronica Dagher and Anne Tergesen spoke for The Wall Street Journal to four retirees in depth about their finances, what gives them joy, and what worries them most. It's hard for us to imagine our future selves, hard to picture what life will be like in retirement, and how we will spend our time and money. For many Americans, retirement advice is limited to encouragement to save more or warnings that they haven't saved enough. But most people get little guidance or give little thought to what to do with all those savings once they reach this next act. People haven't really thought through what retirement is going to look and feel like. They quickly realize they have a lot of time to fill. You need more than a financial plan. The four retirees interviewed live in different parts of the country and are at different phases of life. They offered insight into some of the challenges that retirees — even those with substantial savings — face today. They showed the **importance of having a sense of purpose** in your post-career years and periodically re-evaluating one's needs and desires in response to aging and other changes. (105)

So leading your Third Act with purpose will make your hobbies, travel, gardening, grandkids, etc. better, and you'll be an example for your family of having purpose.

What Does Science Say about Happiness? How Does It Relate to Age?

Many people suffer from a "Great Western Disease." It afflicts those who say or think, "I will be happy when: ... I have a million in the bank... I can move to a bigger house... my children graduate... I retire." But all this is an illusion and one of the most common saboteurs of satisfaction. Goals are then always pushed beyond reach. The Great Western Disease causes us to focus on our dream (and vague, poorly planned future) at the expense of satisfaction with the life we live now. We can be satisfied now. Satisfaction is our choice. What inhibitions to contentment do you have right now? What change are you waiting for in order to be happy? You already have everything you need to be happy. It depends on what part of your brain you use.

When are people the happiest? According to a Happify survey, even if we had happy childhood, it is likely that the level of happiness will grow even more with age. At the age of eighteen, we are typically satisfied with our life. Then the level of happiness gradually decreases until we are in middle age. Around the 53rd year in human life, the level of happiness is the lowest. Work, bringing up children, and paying accounts are all responsibilities that lower our happiness.

But don't despair. **As soon as we get closer to 60, the feeling of happiness grows again**, and many worries diminish. Happiness is **still increasing up to 85** (the oldest age studied), according to the findings. (30) (63)

Well-Being by Age:

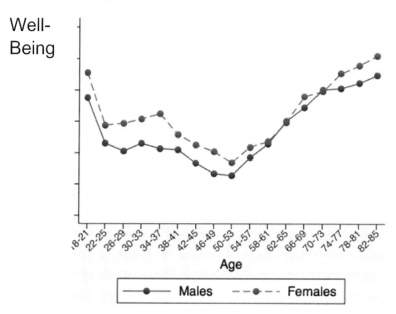

Proceedings of the National Academy of Sciences

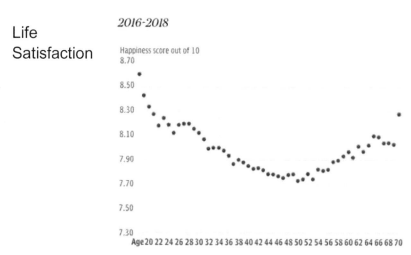

Life satisfaction in the UK CREDIT: PROFESSOR BLANCHFLOWER/NBER

Why are people happier when they grow old? There are several reasons. One of them is the already mentioned fact that happier people live longer, so why frown?

Another discovered reason is the fact that people with increasing age are able to get **much more joy from ordinary little things**. Finally, according to Wes Moss, the author of *You Can Retire Sooner Than You Think*, happy pensioners more often practice volunteering, traveling, or learning new things, which satisfies and fills them. (138)

Because I am already in my Third Act of life, I have noticed enjoyment of little things like good weather, good health, bike trips, relationships with my friends, a good coaching session, and writing this book.

According to a survey by asset manager Abrdn, 54% of those aged over 40 feel anxious about retiring; 61% of those aged 40 to 44 felt anxious. Many respondents said that they felt embarrassed by their lack of knowledge about retirement planning. (34) Psychologist Dr. Linda Papadopoulos: "Retirement anxiety is an emotion of concern or worry experienced by people yet to retire about the prospect of retirement. This could be a concern about how they will fill their time, financial worries, or perhaps feeling a loss of identity. Retiring is one of those big steps we know we'll take at some point in our lives, and we can reduce the risk of 'retirement anxiety' by starting to prepare as early as possible." (79)

Colin Dyer: "Planning for retirement early can help alleviate worries and anxiety, and people shouldn't be embarrassed to raise issues they are not sure or concerned about — it's OK not to know." (79) You may not know much about retirement and pensions. Even if you know people who are retired, they probably don't talk about retirement in detail. So you may simply not know what retirement planning is, let alone how to start.

Advice for all who approach the middle-age: Focus on better perspectives, the ability to retire in full health, and the opportunity to enjoy small beauties and important aspects of life.

Don't hold nostalgia from youth. You have the best years in front of you.

Be sure to imagine the future — in the best possible colors. What do you imagine for a good retirement? Write it down, I'll wait.

_____

_____

_____

_____

_____

_____

_____

_____

_____

_____

You may have a few things come to your mind in that context that may cause concern, and you might like to look for ways to destroy the fear. A lot of people push the topic away (because of fear or because they don't know how to deal with it). Are you one of them? Do you prefer not to think about retirement? Do you think about it regularly? Or are you already taking practical steps? Do you feel strange that you aren't taking enough practical steps to prepare?

_____

_____

_____

_____

_____

_____

_____

_____

_____

Chapter 3: Why Planning for Retirement Seems Difficult

> "You are never given a dream without also being given the power to make it true."   Richard Bach
>
> "People overestimate what they can do in a year but tend to underestimate what they can achieve in ten years."
> Bill Gates

Some reasons for retirement planning difficulty are: We often make job functions and titles our identity, so near retirement people need to positively redefine who they are. And although retirement planning is important, it is not urgent. It requires short-term sacrifices for long-term benefits. Also most people will have to learn which beliefs are sabotaging them and change their beliefs.

In this chapter you will find:
— Why planning for retirement seems difficult
— The relationship between beliefs, thinking, feelings and results
— How reason, autopilot, and reward systems guide the brain
— Why vision, discipline, and consistency are needed
— How differences in approach increase over time

Why Planning for Retirement Seems Difficult

Will Rogers: "It isn't what we don't know that gives us trouble, it's what we know that ain't so."

In our western culture, the question "What do you do?" is more important than who we truly are. We've allowed ourselves to be conditioned by institutions and society. Job functions and titles shape how people are perceived by themselves and others. Career identities hide our true selves. For people who define themselves primarily through their jobs, losing work or retiring is a serious problem. So before or soon after retirement, you should positively redefine who you are. You will live with much more peace of mind and happiness — even without a job. (31)

Plant today. Water. Harvest later.

(Photo: Edward Howell on Unsplash)

Another reason for retirement planning difficulty: Retirement is not an acute problem to solve. The topic is important but not urgent. It will not provide an immediate reward. Just because something is important and not urgent right now doesn't mean you can afford not acting upon it. If you delay, what was not urgent before can become very urgent later on. You will wish then you had acted now.

Retirement planning is emotionally demanding. It requires rational approach with short-term sacrifices for long-term benefits in the future —which often means going against human nature.

Choose to think about preparing for retirement, even when times are not favorable. Usually, if we don't allow ourselves to think about something, there are some worries associated with it. We fear it, so we hide it "safely" inside. So we tend to neglect the topic of retirement planning and preparation.

Your biggest enemies will be **comfort zone trap** (refusal of any change); **learned helplessness** (fear of any loss), i.e., saying "I can't"; and choosing **the path of least resistance** (searching for a quick, easy, and convenient way). (99)

It is time to act. It's never too late to learn — despite widespread opinion.

Michael J. Kami: "Those who do not think about the future cannot have one."

You will have to build new habits. The right habits are hard to build but easy to live with.

George Burns: "I look to the future because that's where I'm going to spend the rest of my life."

Jim Rohn: "We suffer one of two things: either the pain of discipline or the pain of regret. You've got to choose discipline versus regret because discipline weighs ounces and regret weighs tons."

The Relationship between Beliefs, Thinking, Feelings, and Results

Beliefs and awareness | Thinking | Feelings | Actions | Results

Beliefs and awareness lead to thinking, thinking leads to feelings, feelings lead to actions, actions lead to results. (62)

To change our lives, we have to change our beliefs, and to change our beliefs, we have to know which beliefs are sabotaging us ("limiting beliefs"). (59) Develop the habit of being curious about your emotions instead of being carried away with them.

Arthur C. Brooks: "We have the opportunity to change our lives. It just takes a little effort...Change happens when we begin to live our principles instead of being guided by sudden impulses. Then a real moral growth and improvement of quality of life await us."

Many people stick to their old beliefs and hope to get new results —do not be one of them. And it has nothing to do with whether your beliefs are true or not. (Some people are constantly absorbing information that confirms their beliefs = "confirmation bias." Some are even saying, "This is my truth.") Or whether you have all the facts. If you're not careful, you can easily become a product of your environment.

Choose instead the result you are not satisfied with now. Work backward according to the formula above to see which beliefs create the results you don't want. It may feel unnatural first, but with time and practice, your mind will resist it less.

David Robson: "It is possible to push the limits of what we can achieve through a simple change of mindset."

Where do ideas and beliefs come from? They come from what we see, listen to, and read, as well as from past experiences (what we heard, saw, and experienced in childhood). But we have a choice to stop, analyze our thoughts/habits/fears, and not be dragged by old conditioning. No thought lives in us in vain. It either helps or hurts. Let us admit that **our opinions are not part of our self and are not firmly bound to us**. They have no other meaning than that which you attach to them. Don't automatically believe a single one of your thoughts. (59)

Bruce Lipton: "If you want to know which beliefs are sabotaging you, look at your life. Which things come to you easily and gracefully, without much effort? Those are positive beliefs that support those areas of your life. And which areas of your life do you always seem to struggle with? Is it your health or your finances? Is it relationships or your job? Whichever areas of your life you struggle with, you can be 100% sure that you have beliefs, even potentially unconscious to you at the moment, that are causing those areas of your life to suffer."

It's a **common fallacy** for people who get stuck in their belief system, **that their beliefs are unchangeable**. Actually, they're all changeable. **The only thing that doesn't change are your values.** They are your North Star, your constant in life.

Your definition of success and failure should be highly personal. It springs from your inner values, not an external notion of what your life ought to look like. (75)

For example: Imagine a woman having difficulty handling her feelings and a conversation with her husband: "I found out that in the last six months, my husband had lunch with his ex-girlfriend." When I describe this situation, what fairy tales come to mind? Think about it. What extra information did you add? (Was it more than lunch? Did they have dessert? Are they doing something behind her back? Did they rekindle their relationship?) If she starts to feel hurt/jealous, it's because of the story she made up, not because of what she heard. The types of people who are not clear on their beliefs and awareness, or have sabotaging beliefs, often feel offended/hurt (especially in tense situations) and often make up tales that others do what they do because they are evil. These fairy tales lead through feelings to wrong actions and results. (26)

A lady asked how to help her 23-year-old daughter understand that she has to change her habits to get different outcomes. She is always late to work, so she can't hold down a job. She struggles with ADHD, but the lady feels the daughter uses this as an excuse to be unproductive. An expert cites Anne Frank, who once wrote about raising children, "Parents can only give good advice or put them on the right paths, but the final forming of a person's character lies in their own hands." Understanding how habits work can be a huge advantage for anyone wanting to bring about positive change in their life. So forming of the daughter's character lies in her own habits. The definition of habit is "something you do (mentally or physically) that starts as a choice and then becomes a nearly automatic pattern." Simply put, **habits are automatic behaviors.** (107)

Habits are important because they **affect outcomes**. They also affect how we see ourselves and how others see us, and those opinions can open doors and provide opportunities or become barriers to our goals. What does matter is how we see ourselves. The goal for all of us is to build our habits in line with who we want to be. That will drive what we do and lead to what we get.

There are three key factors that will help in this process: belief, outcomes, and behavior.

Belief: To change, we must believe we can change. The lag is the time between when we should change a habit and when we change. The longer we are in the lag, the harder it is to believe we can change. Belief can be fostered by learning how habits work. The daughter is probably experiencing the impact of living in the lag. She may also have a limiting belief related to her diagnosis of ADHD. While it's important to acknowledge and understand limitations, it's equally important to not allow limitations to define her. Her diagnosis doesn't have to define her. It can refine her. Awareness brings choice.

Outcomes: Habits matter when outcomes matter. The daughter wants to be independent and move out on her own. But does she? Is this claim a reflection of what she wants or what she thinks the mother wants? Her current behavior seems to demonstrate the latter. The mother should help her daughter see what the mother is seeing.

James Clear, author of Atomic Habits, writes of what he calls identity-based habits. He says that when habits are tied to our identity, they give us a sense of purpose. More than what we get, it's about who we are, who we want to be, and what we can become. Clear suggests asking the question, **"Who is the type of person that could get the outcome I want?"** (139) Rather than just focusing on the result of living on her own, the mother should help the daughter connect her habits to her identity and her belief in herself, helping her see herself as independent, which will lead to her becoming independent.

Behaviors: If the mother wants to help her daughter identify what she wants to achieve and what kind of person she wants to be, then the mother could ask her what she needs to do on a consistent basis to make those desires a reality. The daughter may not change overnight. The mother can help her make small changes in the things she does most often, identify behaviors of an independent lifestyle that will help her progress and do the things that independent people do, and create small wins and celebrate.

Jim Rohn: "Success is nothing more than a few simple disciplines practiced every day."

For many people it is feasible to start with small wins and build upon them. Small wins become big wins. This can change a big belief. They then believe they can achieve the desired result.

Some people can see what's stopping them is themselves. They can then decide and change a belief instantly. This makes a difference completely — they then change their thinking and actions and get results. They build upon a new belief.

In some cases, the most troublesome things we do in life are basic in nature. However, that sure doesn't mean they are simple.

Success is internally driven. You can't decide exactly how life progresses, but you can choose how you carry yourself through the journey. You create who you want to be, moment by moment. It can sometimes feel like a push to get past these illusionary boundaries. The world will follow what you do and how you do it when you don't back down. (80)

Instead of waiting for permission to raise your standards, you make it happen yourself. All you need to do is step up. Robert Greene once said: "Do not wait for a coronation; the greatest emperors crown themselves." (80)

Earl Nightingale: "We are all self-made, but only the successful will admit it."

Zig Ziglar: "It is your attitude, not your aptitude, that determines your altitude."

☐ **Action step:** Identify your limiting beliefs. Accept you have them, reveal them, realize them, and understand them. The process is best done with somebody.

How Reason, Autopilot, and Reward Systems Guide the Brain

The brain is guided to behave in a certain way by three systems: **reason** (for instance, you already know that you should save for retirement), **autopilot** (learned habits: if something seems to work, there is no need to change it), and the **reward system** (preference for immediate pleasure over future benefits by way of dopamine release). It takes a strong will for reason to prevail. And willpower is stronger and lasts longer the more you believe you have strong willpower and the more you can identify sabotaging beliefs and habits/biases. Hopefully this book will help move you in that direction in retirement planning.

Why Vision, Discipline, and Consistency Are Needed

Unfortunately, a lot of people plan like Brett Favre did (he retired in 2008). After announcing his retirement, he was asked, "What are you looking forward to?" "Nothing," he said. "And I'll stick to that until I do something else."

More relevant here is Joe Girard's quote: "The elevator to success is out of order. You'll have to use the stairs, one step at a time."

An old Japanese proverb: "Vision without action is a daydream. Action without vision is a nightmare."

Petr Ludwig: "Many people have a vision but do nothing to fulfill it. Others are doing but see no vision in their actions. If you have both vision and action, you will get the required emotional and material results."

It is important to have vision and direction in life. You must not back down from them. You must also not be dragged by life events. You have to work on creating them. Without direction, you will find that you are somewhere else completely from where you wanted to be. Ask yourself regularly where you are going, what you want, why, and what the real meaning is. Otherwise, the day will come when you regret your paths. (8)

Giovanni Dienstmann: "Self-discipline is the art of living in harmony with your goals and values...Without self-discipline, the loftiest goal is just wishful thinking. With self-discipline, even a mediocre goal will take you somewhere." (109) To cultivate self-discipline, align your actions with your aspirations and acquire the power you need to achieve them. It helps you resist the diversion of temporary, fleeting enjoyment today at the expense of your future success and happiness.

The more long-term retirement planning is, the more discipline it requires. But it pays off richly. You will struggle with procrastination. Reduce the effects of stress. Take care of your body and mind. You can do it if you reward yourself even for small steps and at the same time don't lose sight of the long-term retirement goal. That is your motivation. Small daily changes can have a compound effect and slowly but surely lead you closer to your goals. (8)

The famous oil billionaire H.L. Hunt once said that only two things actually make a great success. "First, decide exactly what you want." Most people never do. And second, "You have to set a price you're willing to pay to get it. Only then do you decide how to pay it." (99) You can get almost anything you really want if you're willing to pay the price. And usually you pay the full price up front.

The power of tiny steps (James Clear):

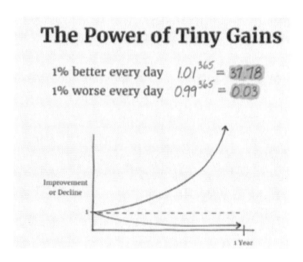

If you get better 1% each day, you are 37 times better in a year. If you get worse 1% each day, you decline to 3% of your original status in a year. (74)

Daily habits create destiny.

You will need discipline, consistency, and momentum.

I read of a lady from LinkedIn who sang a song today that three weeks ago she felt like she had no chance of being able to sing. It was in Italian. It was long. It was high. It was quick. The first time she tried was a disaster, but she approached it by taking small steps.
1.   Learn the Italian words and pronunciation.
2.   Learn the tune without the words.
3.   Decide where to breathe.
4.   Sing the first verse over and over.
5.   Sing the chorus over and over (this was the hardest part).
6.   Sing the second verse over and over.
7.   Sing it all over and over.

Every day she sang this song or some of it. It was so difficult and exhausting that she only sang it for about ten minutes each day to start with. Today, she sang that song pretty well. There is still work to do, but after three consistent weeks of practicing using small steps, she can now sing it.

What do you want to achieve that feels too big and daunting right now? How could you break it down into small steps?

Paul Saffo: "Never mistake a clear view for a short distance."

Here's the story from Paul McCartney's biography Many Years from Now by Barry Miles: "I woke up with a lovely tune in my head. I thought, 'That's great, I wonder what that is?' There was an upright piano next to me to the right of the bed by the window. I got out of bed, sat at the piano, found G, found F sharp… It all leads forward logically. I liked the melody a lot, but because I'd dreamed it, I couldn't believe I'd written it." (140)

That story makes McCartney seem like a creative unicorn who conjured #1 hits from out of nowhere. He isn't, and he didn't. Paul McCartney is talented. He dreamed the melody. You can call McCartney a genius. Just don't call him a born genius. McCartney achieved music greatness because he chose to live and breathe music. He chose to put in the work. He chose to develop his talent.

In his book *Outliers*, Malcolm Gladwell rejects the notion of born geniuses and "prodigies." Those at the top in sports, the arts, and business achieve greatness not because they're prodigies. They achieve greatness because they put in 10,000+ hours to master their craft (about 10 years). He cites the Beatles as an example. Before all the hit records and fame, the Beatles performed regularly in Hamburg. They played more than 1,200 gigs — sometimes 5+ hours a night in Hamburg from 1960 to 1964. By the time they released their first album, they had **10,000+ hours** under their belt. (141)

My friend Jim used to go to gym but could not do so anymore during the pandemic. It took him a commitment to his health to make the next step: a combination of proper nutrition and embracing going for a walk or a swim intentionally. This created releases of dopamine and had self-reinforcing effects. He keeps doing these things every day. This brings direct results. Even if the results are small, they keep building upon each other. And it's not focusing on the result but focusing on the habit, and the habit creates the result. Having great habits creates a sense of wholeness, which he feels from the dopamine release every day. In the long run, it leads to losing weight, better health, and higher satisfaction. And it all started with a commitment and continued with discipline.

Thanks to the power of tiny gains, Third Act planning may not be harder for you. Making your plan is just building small habits. A small bit of attention each day, and you'll hold on to them for a long time. Third Act planning is a marathon, not a sprint. You'll enjoy the process much better.

No matter what stage of life you're in, you can always make changes and benefit from being more intentional with your life.

It's all about belief. But sometimes we have to prove it to ourselves first, and breaking it down into small steps helps to build the belief system so we can achieve the big results. The same principle applies to Third Act planning. (83) You will need consistency. Jobs have built-in consistency, which is why many of us succeed in our careers long term. It's personal goals we suck at the most. Nobody forces you to act. If you don't, there are no immediate consequences. And you can easily cover your inconsistent tracks with various clever excuses. But it is consistency with our personal goals that accounts for much of our success in life. And it's not that consistency is hard. It's just that it's easy to get bored or feel like you're making zero progress and give up. But — remind yourself of the power of tiny steps. Define activities you need to take and make them daily habits. Then build a system around the habits and apply years of patience to it.

Have you experienced success in small steps in your own life?

_____

_____

_____

_____

_____

_____

_____

Can you think about how you can apply the success that you've had in small steps in other parts of your life to the retirement part of your life?

_____

_____

_____

_____

_____

Michael Bungay Stanier: "With small steps, you're doing two things. First, fueled by curiosity, you're collecting feedback... Second, you're mitigating risk."

How Differences in Approach Increase over Time

Satisfied old age: If you don't want to, you don't have to change your habits, social ties, relationships, or work habits. The system does not support it much. It forgets people over 60 or creates stereotypes (ageism). The senior age is from 65 years, and the differences (not only medical) between people are large. It's up to us how we live, how we work with ourselves, how we keep fit (physically, mentally, socially, or spiritually), and how we have sorted it out in our heads. Everything will show and add up in old age. An active 70-year-old usually has the fitness of a passive 50-year-old.

Once you decide to take full responsibility for your retirement preparation, you will often have to go against your instincts (called "cognitive limitations" (5)). Most of the major steps outlined later in my book add up exponentially over time. That's why they are counterintuitive. (The brain can see linear trends, not exponential ones.)

Arthur E. Morgan: "Preparation for old age should begin no later than one's teens. A life which is empty of purpose until 65 will not suddenly become filled on retirement."

Karen Lamb: "A year from now you may wish you had started today."

Although some people are already motivated to do something, they often underestimate the preparation. In general, we should not wait for crises to become a catalyst for change because then we would only be responding to what is happening to us in life. Even worse are those who do not even try to change because they are often forced to change by a crisis, such as a large drop in income upon retirement or a decline in physical or mental freshness relatively soon after retirement.

Typically, if we allow the crisis to be a catalyst for change, we only respond to things that happen to us in life. We just glue and fix things. (13) In the case of retirement, however, we will no longer have enough time or energy to resolve the crisis. It is all the more important to take life into your own hands now and actively start to change yourself. Be an active creator of your own life both now and for your Third Act.

Some build great power or a great career or company during their work life. Some strive for fame or see meaning in hard work or in wealth. What will you use it for? You probably have an idea that one day it all may pass away, that retirement is coming. Keep that in mind and get ready for it.

Unknown: "The best time to start thinking about your retirement is before your boss does."

Mark Twain: "Age is an issue of mind over matter. If you don't mind, it doesn't matter."

Did you used to see planning for retirement as difficult? Have you identified any belief(s) that are sabotaging you? Are you ready to change your reason, autopilot, and reward system? Do you have vision and discipline? Have you experienced success in small steps for a long time in your own life?

Do you ever talk to your friends about what it will be like in retirement, that doesn't only include travel? What about the rest of the time that you're not traveling?

Chapter 4: The Supporting Pillars of Your Third Act Preparation

> "We should think more about who we will be in the future because it has profound implications for our health, happiness, and financial security." David Robson

I have explained why retirement preparation is important. There are several variables influencing the quality of your Third Act. I group them in four "pillars."

This chapter will answer:
— What are the four pillars?
— Should you start preparing goals for your Third Act?
— What are some first Action Steps?
— What are the features of good goals?

What Are the Four Pillars?

It seems there are only six variables that matter when we face retirement: health, wealth, relationships, meaning, contribution, and happiness. Meaning, contribution, and happiness are closely related. The happiest rentiers still contribute to the world, seek meaning in what they do, and seek contentment in what they do today — not on what they used to be. So I have four basic variables, or pillars, as shown below. We will discuss these pillars in more detail in the next chapters.

HEALTHY, WEALTHY, AND HAPPY RETIREMENT

STRATEGY

FINANCE

HEALTH

SOCIAL

LIFESTYLE

WHY THIS IS IMPORTANT

What measure of physical, mental, social, lifestyle, and financial fitness would you like to have in your retirement years?

What are you doing about it today?

These two questions apply whether you are now in your thirties and working full-time or in your sixties and fully retired.

Think about life after work. How can you contribute? How can you find meaning? What will please you? What will provide you with the best experiences? You may have 20-30 or more years left. How will this time be important for you and the people around you? Now is a good time to start planning.

Decide today that you accept full responsibility for the preparation for your Third Act. Don't complain about anyone or anything, whether to yourself or others or circumstances or situations.

You are responsible. You can choose to change your mind. You can decide to change your approach. This book should help.

George Bernard Shaw: "Those who cannot change their mind cannot change anything."

Andy Storch encourages us in his book to find ways to take positive action, even when circumstances seem out of your control. When something bad or unexpected occurs, you may feel tempted to think of yourself as a victim of circumstances beyond your control. While many things in life are beyond your control, thinking of yourself as a victim breeds inaction. (75) I strongly believe you can always look for the things you can control. The longer we live, the more the list of things that can happen to us in life grows. They are opportunities to either be a victim and blame others (or the Universe) or to take responsibility and have a belief that **everything happens for us, not to us**.

Taking responsibility for your circumstances means avoiding excuses and finger pointing. Start practicing this behavior now: stop complaining about anything and everything for 30 days and see how you feel. Instead, start considering what unexpected events makes possible and what you might learn from them. It is shifting your mindset from negative to positive. Learn from the experience, adapt your plans, and move forward. Brainstorm ways you can take greater responsibility for your life.

A purposeful man planted a tree. For the next 40 years he watered it, protected it from harsh weather, and never picked its fruit. He did not take a break to rest in its shade. He never went anywhere or did anything else because he focused solely on growing that tree bigger and bigger. One day, just after his 65th birthday, the tree stopped growing.

He looked up at its big trunk and widespread branches and said to himself: "What was that for?" (34)

Many people spend first act years in preparation for the second act, then have a successful second act, but do not plant and water their financial retirement tree for their Third Act at all. Others treat their retirement financial planning in a similar way as the purposeful man above. Their work is only about growing the tree. They never think about harvesting one day to make a better Third Act for themselves. As long as the tree keeps growing, they never think of the higher purpose. Their sense of purpose was so connected to working hard to make more money that they may delay retirement as long as they physically can to make money they don't really need and will never spend.

Others live very conservatively and never enjoy their retirement because they're concerned about running out of money. There is a purpose to having money and growing the wealth tree, but what money can't do is create purpose in and of itself. You want your Third Act to be a time to stop worrying, as your financial tree is ready. You'll be able to live comfortably off the money you've saved and the income that your investments will generate. After a lifetime of working hard and following your financial plan, your return on investment will be financial security in retirement. And you will be able to live the best life possible with the money you will have.

You need not wait until you reach your Third Act. You can start harvesting the tree a bit each year and enjoy life today, while still growing it for the future. Enjoying life along the way will make your eventual transition to the Third Act even easier. With a good strategy, you'll be ready to gradually give even more of your time and energy into the activities that really matter to you.

Start Preparing Goals for Your Third Act Plan

George Carlin: "Some people have no idea what they're doing, and a lot of them are really good at it."

Brian Tracy: "Success is goals, and all else is commentary."

Imagine yourself in ideal retirement. Where are you? Who are you there with? What do you do? How do you feel? What do you see? What is another option where you would like to be? How do you feel there? What does an ideal day look like? What do you do for 24 hours in retirement if you have enough money, time, and you don't have to do anything? What about a week? A month?

☐ **Action step:** Write down right now what your ideal retirement looks like.

_____

_____

_____

_____

(You will be expanding on it later in this book in each of the following chapters.)

Start preparing your Third Act goals. Even if you don't feel ready yet, write a short statement — a first draft — describing your purpose at a high level and a first version of your Third Act goals. Don't aim for perfection at this stage; you will revise and expand on them later — both while reading this book and during your life.

Get a separate sheet of paper. Write them down. Believe me, writing down your goals is important. (They will find their way into your subconscious; everyday small decisions will then move you toward them, and it will increase your self-discipline.)

What about you? Do you have your goals written down, or do you carry them around in your head? If you do the exercises in writing, you will be in the top three percent of people, and your chances of success will increase even more. Good! You have separated yourself from the majority of people who cannot resist the feeling of laziness in life and prefer to carry their goals in their heads, rather than take pen and paper and write them down. (99). I once wondered how much power writing goals has and have found the greatest things happen between pen and paper.

You may want to download and use the template List of Goals.xlsx from **www.livingyourbestthirdact.com**.

☐ **Action step:** Think about and write it down: "Which one knowledge, if you acquired it and used it excellently, would have the greatest positive impact on your retirement life and preparation for it?" (16)   Add this to your goals with high priority.

_____

_____

_____

Confucius: "When it is obvious that the goals cannot be reached, don't adjust the goals. Adjust the action steps."

☐ **Action step:** review your goals under PEVS guidelines:
— **P**ositive,
— **E**xciting and Emotional (you really want it),
— **V**isualized,
— unrealistic = a little **S**cary.

This framework will help your goals become motivating and get you out of thinking too small. It will stretch your talents and capabilities, take you out of your comfort zone, and create a sense of urgency. Your goal(s) has to be so audacious that there is a possibility you might not achieve it. You're aiming for the stars; if you miss, you will land on the moon.

Joe Vitale: "A goal should scare you a little and excite you a lot."

Michael Bungay Stanier: "We unlock our greatness by working on the hard things."

Here are the **elements of a good PEVS goal**:
— It's positive
— You see a clear picture of the future state
— Feels as if it's 70% achievable
— Has to be clear and compelling
— You think "I want" and not "I should"
— Expands your current capabilities
— Must be connected to your strategy
— Is long-term, probably a minimum of 10 years or longer

Affirmations, accountability, and coaching, among other strategies, can help you achieve your goals. In addition to strategies like PEVS, utilize other tools to achieve your vision.

One helpful tool is daily affirmations. A useful affirmation reminds you of something true about yourself or reminds you of your main goals. Hiring a professional coach or joining a "mastermind group" can provide much-needed support and prompt you to push yourself harder.

You may want to consider using some of these tools:
— Write a letter to your future self (https://www.future me.org/)
— Reflect on the past period and plan the next one (https://yearcompass.com/)

Don't worry about perfection. Doing something is always better than doing nothing.

My friend Jim and his wife realized they should not speak and think of financials only. They discussed what kind of a lifestyle they are looking to have. Financial goals come when they know what kind of a lifestyle they want to have, which is related to their purpose. And that conversation doesn't happen only one time. As they grow, it's a consistent conversation. Their vision and lifestyle adjust to who they are.

Andy Storch: "One of the biggest things that separate those who achieve big success from those who don't is action."

Chapter 5: Your Financial Plan for Retirement

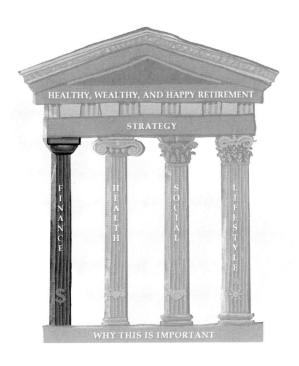

> "You can be young without money, but you can't be old without it." Tennessee Williams

Can you imagine running out of money in your Third Act of life and being too old or no longer able to earn some? How much do you want to rely on the status of the Social Security system (or an employer-provided pension plan, if you have one) in retirement?

Your Mission for this chapter — should you choose to accept it — is to prepare and start implementing a Retirement Action Plan to get retirement wealth on autopilot, so that you can have a wealthy retirement — when the time comes. Imagine retiring financially secure, so you can live as a rentier[1] for decades. Also imagine doing what you have planned for, when you want, with whom you want, wherever you want, for as long as you want, when retired.

After reading this chapter you will understand:
— The steps for your financial plan preparation
— The details of those steps
— The history and future of pension and Social Security systems
— How to get rid of toxic money beliefs
— Preparation steps hints
— The relationship between money and happiness
— The new map of life
— Your potential financial strategy for the Third Act
— What Action Steps you should take

The Steps For Your Financial Plan Preparation

By understanding the context (history and future of pension and Social Security systems), building the preparation basics, planting your wealth tree (9-Action-Step system to create your retirement financial plan), and watering the wealth tree, you will be prepared to retire financially secure, so you can do almost anything you want.

---

1   Living on income from your savings and investments

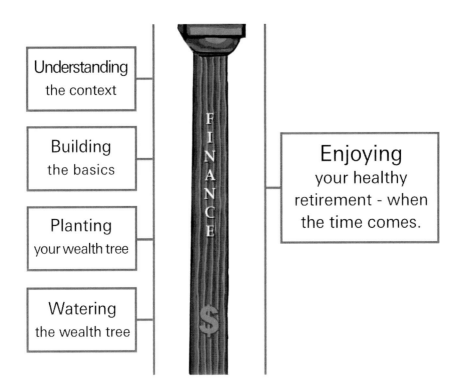

| Understanding the context |
| Building the basics |
| Planting your wealth tree |
| Watering the wealth tree |

FINANCE

Enjoying your healthy retirement - when the time comes.

The History and Future of Pensions / Social Security

You probably know and expect that government pensions or social systems (called Social Security Administration (SSA) in the U.S., other names in other countries) mean a substantial reduction in living standards. How much can you (or do you want to) rely on a government or employer-provided pension plan in retirement? How much do you want (or need) to save or invest? With what savings and assets (which are fully under your control, out of reach of the government, children, etc.) do you want to retire?

If any commercial investment product were as unreliable as the pension system, central banks as regulators would have banned it a long time ago. Let alone if the government as a "provider" changed it as arbitrarily as some countries do. Yet, people pay big contributions. And in many countries no one has a concrete idea how their "insurance premiums" will translate into the amount of income the state will pay them in retirement for many decades. Anytime you rely on the government to handle your money, you can expect problems. Consider pensions as a nice bonus, but don't count on them to live on.

According to a Rutgers University study, 76% of baby boomers want to retire before 60, but only 29% think they will have enough money. A 2022 survey by RetireOne and Midland National Life shows that concerns and fears regarding retirement goals are up for real debate. According to the surveyed advisors:
— 80% of clients are worried that Social Security won't be sufficient
— 73% said clients are unsure about protecting income in retirement
— 64% said clients aren't convinced they'll retire on time (84)

Among American households ages 45 to 54, 42% do not have any retirement savings, and the median retirement balance is only $100,000. (86)

The time will come when you realize you have worked all your life and no longer want to worry financially when you retire. If you don't prepare properly, it may easily happen that you'll be nearly out of money and too old or incapable of making any. Ideally, you will not have to continue working (unless you want to). Do you plan on relying on the state pension or employer-provided pension plan to do that?

Pension plans and Social Security systems have long been heading to huge deficits. This is not a problem exclusive to just one country but to most countries. All of them have very similar challenges. You can't count on Social Security systems, not only because their rules change depending on what's going on in a particular country. There are also deeper, more global reasons: demographic trends (too many people in the system and not enough funds); social, economic, populist, and political trends now significantly strengthened by pandemic effects, and possibly an impact of the war in Ukraine.

Partial modifications to current systems cannot help. It is a huge problem that is not being talked about much right now. But that does not reduce its size. Quite the contrary. The population-strong generations will start retiring soon in many countries. Thanks to governments' attitudes, we will be in a situation where we will have to control debt and stabilize public budgets in a time when we are already intensively confronted with the effects of population aging. It's a worldwide issue. In your particular country, you are going to experience somewhat different forms of it. Deficits will be unmanageable between 2030 and 2050 in different countries, and nearly no government is treating it now. I will say in a moment what you can do with it personally and how to plan.

The first big opportunity for the state to invest in future pensions was many decades ago. It did not happen in most countries. Previous governments have since failed to prepare full pension reform. For instance, it's been 30 years and 5 pension commissions with no result in my country. Ideally the pension account should be separated from the state budget (so being out of reach of momentary political decisions) and originally it had been the case in some countries.

No tax reform, pension reform, health, or education reform. The short-term horizon prevailed in the decisions of many governments, but we'll all feel the long-term effects. Not only is nothing saved, but we also have an ongoing PAYG system, where there are fewer and fewer workers contributing to current retirees.

These mandatory expenditures are an increasing burden on the state budget (now increased by the pandemic and economic slowdown). For instance, mandatory expenditures were 60% of the federal budget in the U.S. in FY 2020. In my country, it was 84% of the state budget (42% for social security benefits). Germany used 51% for social security benefits in 2015. This decreases the principles of solidarity in many countries, and often the system is so extreme, that "the line between contributions and taxes is blurred" for high earners, as OECD experts had to conclude. Moreover the budget for future pensions will be very limited. Also, individual pension support mostly has not received any big attention and will no longer receive any. It is too late for reforms now. Governments have been preparing pension reforms for so long that the population has aged in the meantime. Now there are only two things left to do, which are both unpopular: parametric adjustments to the state pension pillar and greater support and popularization of voluntary pension saving. This is true in most developed countries of the world.

Edward Prescott, Nobel Prize winner in economics (died in November 2022 at 81), gave this recommendation to the government in my country in 2005: "You should cut taxes. When you take into account social security payments, your taxes are still high." The government did not listen, quite the opposite. They implemented the "flat tax," followed by a tax rate decrease to 15% in 2020. This led to state revenue erosion at the most inconvenient time. (97)

Prescott also criticized dependence on state pensions. In his lecture "How to pay for an aging society" in 2005, he recommended both more merit-based pay-as-you-go system and mandatory investment of about a tenth of income in funds. The government then introduced a very cautious "second social security pillar," which was canceled soon by the subsequent government. The dependence on flat-rate pensions has not disappeared, and it is becoming increasingly clear that the system is not financeable with the current parameters. We will know this at the latest when the generation born in the 1970s applies for pensions. Thanks to the pandemic and subsequent impacts of the war in Ukraine, we can see it even now.

The solution could be a combination of later retirement (it will certainly come, no matter how often politicians deny it); a reduction in the pension-to-wage ratio (replacement rate), which is already happening in my country (46% in 1993, under 40% in 2017); and further reduction in the merit of most equal pensions in Europe and some other countries. Other possible "solutions" include government debt; inflation; higher labor taxation; higher additional levies; higher excise duties (which means mainly alcohol, cigarettes and gasoline); higher taxation of real estate, property, and capital; and possibly an increase of VAT.

The partial solution may also be a system of incentives for people to either have children or contribute to savings. Or we will roll the debts in front of us with the help of central banks and artificially low rates, creating large accompanying bubbles (real estate, stock, and so on). I don't want to think about how it was solved in the past (war) or elsewhere (state bankruptcy). Politicians will not tell you because people do not want to hear it. These are problems that will affect future generations. In the past, politicians occasionally warned that the pay-as-you-go system could not provide us with decent pensions as the population aged but did nothing to change it. The only change is they mostly do not mention this issue anymore. The same is true with health care, social care, and tax reform in many countries.

As an example: Many older Japanese can no longer afford to stop working as demographic woes pressure the nation's labor market and social security system. The Ministry of Internal Affairs in Japan announced that those age 75 and older accounted for more than 15% of the total population for the first time, and the ratio of those over 65 hovered at a record 29.1% — the highest in the world. That figure is expected to reach 38.4% by 2065. Meanwhile, the number of over-65s with jobs grew for its 18th consecutive year, hitting 9.09 million, or 13.5% of the working population. And when looking at those between the ages of 65 and 69, more than 50% are working. The percentage of those age 60 and over in paid employment who wished to continue working was 40.2% in Japan, higher than the three other nations surveyed: the United States, Germany, and Sweden.

The government emphasizes the "100-year-life" and pushes for related labor market reforms aimed at allowing people to work well into their twilight years. Businesses are required to secure opportunities for their employees to work until they reach 70. Prime Minister Fumio Kishida laid out his growth strategy, with one of his pillars aimed at "putting to rest people's anxiety about the era of 100-year lifespans." (97) Whether he succeeds remains a question.

My conclusion: The state will not take care of you in the long run with enough dignity. You have to think about it for yourself. It's many years of your life. You're responsible for yourself. So a good strategy is to be dependent as little as possible on the state, politicians, and their decisions. I'll say more on this later.

Details of Building the Basics/Your Money Mindset

☐ **Action step: Add the relevant tasks to your list of goals** when reading the text.

Why is your money mindset so important? What you think about money and how you talk about money is as important as what you do with your money. Your money mindset is so important because it is what directs everything you do with your money.

Money has a lot of emotional load around it. Money beliefs can hold you back unnecessarily. They can make you have a harder time, especially in your Third Act. If you make a mistake during your second act, you have the advantage of often having a chance to make it back, as you have the rest of your life to do that. This isn't so later in the Third Act. So pay attention to the words you say and see if you relate to any of the toxic money beliefs. What comes out of our mouths is what is going on in our minds, which creates an energy that is sent off to the word. And what you put out is what you receive.

A belief system is often created out of habits. It usually comes from parents or people around you. Your unconscious will take over when you're not aware of it. That hurts you in all phases of your life.

Build the right mindset instead and get better every day. You may think of money as spiritual energy and use it to your benefit.

Start with being aware that you have negative beliefs. The energy that you have from negative beliefs will hold you back, especially in the area of money. Realize that beliefs can be changed.

If you find yourself saying in a conversation or to yourself, "Money is evil," as soon as you realize it, immediately think "Cancel, cancel, cancel" or "Five, four, three, two, one." Now think a positive thing (empowering belief) instead, e.g. "Money is good and serves my purpose." You have to work on it and change consciously. The deep-seated habit affects you in a profound way. Turn it around. Continue to use this technique. By changing the meaning of something, it changes the results at the end.

Also, never use "I am" in a non-supportive role, e.g. "I'm not good with money." Use "I am increasingly getting better with money" instead. What happens then is you cannot help but work on it.

William Arthur Ward: "If you can imagine it, you can achieve it. If you can dream it, you can become it."

Some toxic money beliefs are:

—   "Money is evil" or "I'm not good with money." If you think money is evil, you do everything to have no money. The truth is that money is good if you made it legally and honestly and use it to do good. And everyone can learn to get better with money or seek support and help.

—   "I'll be happy only when I'm making more money." We're always in the waiting room, assuming that we will be happy if we achieve a certain income goal. The truth is that you can be happy now even if you don't have a million bucks in the bank. And regarding Third Act preparation, I recommend being self-aware in both time horizons (happy now and happy then).

- "You need a business to achieve financial freedom." Many motivational speakers advocate "very few people can become millionaires by being an employee." The truth is that you really don't need to be a full-time entrepreneur. Financial freedom is all about having options. For example, having multiple income streams, like part-time entrepreneurship, selling online courses, rental properties, and passive investments. Or you could do the same work as a contractor. There are many ways to achieve your money goals. And you can have multiple streams of income. Don't let people on the internet tell you there's only one way to do something.

- "Money is more important than my time." Everything we do has an opportunity cost. Always think of the cost of the time you may have wasted, e.g. to get a cheaper option. And do not throw money at your problems. It's common when we're stressed or unful-filled. Instead, try to be self-aware and find the root cause of these issues. That's a better way to spend one's time.

- "Money doesn't grow on trees." This belief puts us in a scarcity mindset. But building sustainable wealth isn't about holding on tightly to the small amount of money we make. You can rather concentrate on creating value. The truth is that you can generate money from nothing as long as you have the skills to provide value that other people will pay for. (71)

Toxic money belief	Empowering belief
Money is evil.	Money is good if you made it legally and honestly. I use money in positive ways. I am a lover of money and all it can do for me, my family, and the world around me.

I'm not good with money.	I am a lifelong learner of money. I am increasingly getting better with money each day. I am wealthy. I manage my money well. I don't blame others for my failures.
I just get by. I'm not rich.	I am rich beyond my dreams. I am wealthy in all areas of my life, especially financial, and I love it.
I can start being happy only when I'm making more money.	I have a positive attitude. I am happy now. I am happy in my Third Act. I have a complete, full life that I deserve and desire.
I need a business to achieve financial freedom.	There are more ways to achieve my money goals. Financial freedom is all about having options. I look for multiple streams of income.
Money is more important than my time.	I am a master of both my time and my money.
Money doesn't grow on trees.	My money continuously grows.
I'm swept through life by chance and fate.	I make my own life.
I'm playing not to lose.	I'm playing to win.
I want to be rich.	I am determined and committed to work for my wealth. I focus on what I want.

I see obstacles.	I focus on the opportunities. Obstacles are my milestones.
I hate other rich people.	I admire other wealthy people. I learn from other rich people.
My friends are pessimistic.	I'm friends with successful, optimistic people.
I let my problems get in the way.	I am bigger than my problems. I know success is always there.
I have trouble receiving.	I can give but also receive.
I keep track of my income.	I keep track of my assets.
I work for my money.	My money works for me.
I let my fear paralyze me.	I act even when I'm scared. I feel the fear and do it anyway (calculated risks).
I think I know everything.	I am still learning. I am a lifelong learner of money.

Based on (62), (71)

Keep challenging your beliefs. Create a supporting belief system.

Many people carry bad habits from act one and fortify them in act two. Now when approaching your Third Act or in your Third Act or planning for the Third Act, unless you do something, you will be taking all that baggage with you. This makes not only your financial status worse but other pillars as well. You can have the intention of wanting to change your life or prepare for your Third Act, but if your belief system does not support that, you will not find success, and you will struggle. This chapter is not just about numbers. Please understand that to really accomplish what you desire in your plan, you'll need to do more than just follow a set of rules. You'll need consistency.

"You can be anything or anyone you want, just act like it." - Charles Duhigg, *The Power of Habit*

☐ **Action step:** As you go throughout your day, watch for a toxic money belief you have. Which beliefs are having the greatest negative impact? What is it costing you? Take note, and when you're in a relaxed, calm space, write down what would be the empowering belief. What impact would this new belief have on your finances? Practice it. Say the toxic money-belief, interrupt yourself and say, "Cancel, cancel, cancel. Five, four, three, two, one." Say your empowering belief. When you say a toxic money belief habitually later, you will be aware and can interrupt it. Then replace it with something powerful. How will you know when your beliefs have changed? What behavioral changes would you expect to see? Communication with yourself is integral to success (as it dictates the actions you will take).

Fill in your toxic belief and empowering belief here:

_____

_____

_____

_____

Henry Ford: "Whether you think you can, or you think you can't, you're right."
Marcus Aurelius: "People are not disturbed by things but by the views they take of them."

He who acts correctly must have been thinking correctly before.
Many times, when you change one part of your life, it affects another. My friend sold his share of his business and

immediately transitioned into his new career. He was very uncomfortable because of the strong habit he had of always going to the same place to work for 18 years. Now he felt useless, even though he had started the other business and had been doing it for a more than year as a side hustle. He had to find some sort of area of life that he could work on while figuring it out.

Instead of sitting at home twiddling his thumbs and not knowing what to do, he went to the gym every time he woke up and felt bored. He brought his phone, notepad, and pen. He found that when his focus wasn't on business but on something like going to the gym and working out, it raised his level of energy and was attracting positivity to him. Raising up his physical realm affected all the other areas of his life — relationships, financials and business, social, and spiritual. I am getting similar effects from trips to the woods and mountains, either walking, cycling, cross-country skiing, etc.

Sometimes, you might feel like you have to control every part of your life, but actually, just by changing one part of it, in this case changing your beliefs around money, you can change all the other aspects of your life. Everything gets better when we work on an area that maybe we haven't put enough time into or have a negative energy coming from it. You may think this chapter is only about money, but it's not just about money. Money is energy, and we need to treat it just like any other energy and feed it with positivity in the direction that we want to go. Create an environment that promotes this belief system. Things will come to you because you will be ready to accept them.

Preparation Steps Hints

Get an overview of your debts.

Create a plan to pay off your debts on time. (You can seek an independent expert for advice should you need to.)

The crucial mistake 99% of people make is increasing their expenses as they increase their income. The problem is known as "lifestyle inflation."

Will Rogers: "Too many people spend money they haven't earned, to buy things they don't want, to impress people that they don't like."

Thomas Stanley & William Danko: "Allocating time and money in the pursuit of looking superior often has a predictable outcome: inferior economic achievement. What are three words that profile the affluent? FRUGAL FRUGAL FRUGAL." (160)

To save money, you must identify where the money is wasted. (76) Get rid of the mindless money wasters some people think are acceptable:

— All sorts of products designed to make us look good. The global beauty industry has skyrocketed from $483B in 2020 to $511B in 2021 and is expected to hit $716B by 2025. (76) There's no need to spend a fortune on looking good.
— If you are gambling or speculating (in any form), stop it. The odds are against you.
— Paying somebody too much to tell you how to work out. You can find free workout routines online. You may want to pay someone to prevent you from giving an excuse not to exercise.
— Expensive vacations you will not remember. Always consider the price against the experience and memories the vacation will give you.
— In some countries, cable companies are too expensive. The average American pays $217 per month ($2600 per year) for TV service. (76) Do you really need all these channels (and commercials)?
These examples are just the tip of the iceberg when it comes to mindless money wasters. **Don't let your ego do your buying.**

When you see a luxury car or SUV on the road, it's probably not driven by a millionaire. Many people who live in expensive homes and drive luxury cars do not actually have much wealth. The truly wealthy know that the thrill of buying a luxury car, a suit, a watch, or any other high-status artifact lasts about a month, but the pride of buying assets and increasing financial independence lasts a lifetime (160).

Improve your financial education. In many families in Western Europe, investing is rooted in their behaviors. Some children see their parents take care of finances wisely. In adulthood, they imitate them. Don't forget that you are ultimately responsible for yourself.

Don't be afraid to **ask for** and **receive help**. Most people don't achieve their goals on their own. They do it with help. Why does it sometimes feel so difficult to ask for help? You may worry that receiving help makes you look less capable or successful, but most people enjoy helping others and won't look down on you for asking. Sometimes, asking for one thing leads to something even better.

There are so many people and places that can help you on your journey. The biggest key is to get over your ego and stop thinking you should be able to figure everything out. (75)

Change your beliefs and thinking about money. Remove your money blocks. Develop a wealthy mind. Talk to people who want to see you succeed. If many others can do it, you can, too.

Philosopher Alan Watts: "By replacing the fear of the unknown with curiosity, we open ourselves up to an infinite stream of possibility."

Curiosity means to try something new, to learn something new, to nudge the edge of your comfort zone, and introduce variety.

Decide to save for retirement. The younger you are, the less you have to sacrifice to reach the same end amount. Invest your savings. **Have a strategy.** When you seek help, believe there is **no free help.** Find out what the advisor is profiting from.[2] And check their **credibility,** e.g. will they still be around in two years?

---

2 Financial consulting generally works in the mode of "commission consulting" (mediation of financial products). For the client, the services appear to be "free." But the reality is that financial advisers get commissions from financial institutions on the products you have bought from them. So it's not free. It's just that these fees were hidden from you and often hard to read for the advisors themselves. These fees are often quite high. (The financial institution shares the commission with the advisor and with other intermediaries, and ultimately it must be paid itself.) This is common practice for insurance underwriters, bank staff, or estate agents. Almost all of them are dependent on commissions from the business, and this forces them to sell more and more products, even if you don't need it, don't want it, or just aren't interested. (https://buff.ly/3rKz3nn)

Many people, small companies, and municipalities had their money managed by a small German bank (Volksbank) in my country. In 2012, Volksbank was acquired by a big Russian bank (Sberbank). This was also a very well managed and healthy bank. But in 2022, Sberbank fell under sanctions thanks to the war in Ukraine. The Guarantee Fund reimbursed individual clients fully, but 180 municipalities will lose most or all of their money. The local politicians were not cautious enough since 2014 when Russia invaded Ukraine and did nothing since then.

First lesson: common sense urged a redirection of savings and other business relationships away from Sberbank. Those who did not, did not respect the need to diversify risk. Second lesson: it is important to evaluate all information well before making any big decision. And this is often not possible without external support from competent experts. Many people are ready to pay a plumber or a roofer but do not properly value advice from professionals such as financial experts, lawyers, or IT experts. This attitude can cost them a lot more money in the long run. In this case, if municipalities had good and responsible advisors, they would not have lost billions of crowns.

When markets fall, emotions often run high. They force us to react to the situation. But these are exactly the moments when the success or failure of our investment strategy is written. If you invest on your own, remind yourself of the reasons you built your portfolio the way you did. Do not react to the situation. If you invest with the help of a (carefully selected) professional portfolio manager (financial asset manager), believe them. In either case, this can help: like your portfolio. If you like something, it's hard to get rid of it. Have a couple of investments in your portfolio that are close to your heart that you really believe in.

Use a healthy degree of **vigilance**. The first question should not be what to invest in but "How can I increase my regular monthly savings?" Set aside as much as possible. **Learn not to waste money and manage it wisely.** Gain at least basic knowledge and habits. Think about your normal living expenses and how much of them could be saved and invested. Think primarily about spending on housing, transportation, and food. **Make a monthly budget.** There's a lot on the web on this, for example: https://medium.com/makingofamillionaire/how-to-track-where-your-money-is-going-548f014428be. Add this to your list of goals.

Nearly every millionaire in a study saved a minimum of 15% of their annual income. If 15% seems impossible, upload your credit and debit card spending into a budgeting app that breaks out your discretionary spending, and you'll quickly see opportunities to spend less while maintaining your quality of life. Whatever area of discretional spending you see as an opportunity for saving money (eating out, entertainment, travel, hobbies, gadgets, home decor, and anything else beyond your basic needs), make a budget for it and stick to it (160).

Experts say people should **follow three basic** tips when investing: **diversify, don't gamble, and rebalance** (respond to changes in the value of individual assets). Ignore the media headlines. Ignore the current ups and downs of stock markets in terms of speculating when to jump into investments. (72) Market timing does not work. (77) As a small investor, invest as soon as the money comes. Procrastination can be worse than bad timing. Long term, it's almost always better to invest in stocks — even at the worst time each year — than not to invest at all. If you aren't psychologically resistant to downturns, divide the sums prepared into smaller chunks and invest them gradually. Statistics show that it is best to build a portfolio (or have one built), clearly define your rules, and ignore various "expert" recommendations and short-term market fluctuations.

I hesitated to invest during good times in the market many years ago, believing it would be even better later. Thinking of investing in bad times is even more counterintuitive. So I have procrastinated again. And by doing so, I have missed one of the short time periods of big growth. I know now such periods improve the portfolio performance for years ahead. As no one can predict such periods, procrastination is not a good strategy.

The **inability to delay gratification** is the number one reason most people will not be wealthy. Making money is more about reinforcing timeless lessons rather than learning new ones. Sprint, if possible, but understand that this game is a marathon. Making money fast is possible, but making money easy is not. (66)

Money can give you control over your time. As a young adult, you have time and health but no money. In mid-life, you have money and health but no time. In later life, you have money and time but no health. **Can you break the third rule?** (66)

Money is a system, not a goal. Tim Denning: "**Millionaires have goals. They turn them into habits. Habits form systems. Systems create financial automation.**" (110) What percent of your monthly income do you save? What percent do you invest? What percent do you spend? Once you're comfortable with how much you save and invest, automate. **The best systems don't rely on willpower.**

Use the money lessons to win the game. And once you've won the game, use your self-awareness to know when to stop playing.

When you have reasonable savings, **don't bet on "miracle" instruments**. (There is no holy grail.) Forget NFTs[3] and crypto. Always consider **risk**[4] **, return, and liquidity** with every investment. You can hardly find an optimum combination in any single asset. Retirement money should best be **diversified** (different instruments, different geographies, different currencies, etc.). I recommend not studying too much around it. Rather, find

---

3 NFT, non-fungible token, is a record on a blockchain which is associated with a particular digital or physical asset, typically digital files such as photos, videos, and audio. It is a virtual ownership. The ownership of an NFT can be transferred by the owner, allowing NFTs to be sold and traded. You may want some gamification of a little bonus money; you might want to invest in something silly.

4 The typical textbook says the higher the volatility of a given asset, the higher its riskiness. That may be a misunderstanding of risk. Risk should be determined by the investor in the form of **a goal to maintain the real value** of money. Cash does not automatically make it possible to achieve that objective because it will never hold its real value. From this perspective, cash is extremely risky because you will never achieve your goal. But in economic theory, it is risk-free because it does not fluctuate. Stocks, on the other hand, are considered risky because of high volatility, which is paradoxical because their chances of holding their real value are higher than in the case of cash. (50)

a good and truly **independent investment advisor** (portfolio manager). Accept that if they are to be truly independent, **you will pay them** in some form.

An independent portfolio manager will create a plan for you based on detailed knowledge of your situation, needs, and the lifecycle stage you are in now (hence your risk appetite). They will use any necessary tools (bonds, stocks, ETFs, funds of all types, and many more) in the right proportion and keep it up to date as market conditions change. They put a lot of analytical work into it, so they charge you, but it's well worth investing.

I selected my portfolio manager decades ago. They have saved my portfolio during two financial crises already and are making reasonable profits in good times. I am paying them a fixed fee and sometimes a success fee. It is OK because they are the experts, and they do the analytical work every day to know what to do with their clients' money. They have tools, knowledge, and insight that would never be available to me as an individual investor.

It takes years, decades, to build up sufficient reserves. Good advice is to invest regularly for several decades.[5]

There are times that you do get windfalls. Use these windfalls as an opportunity to add to your investment portfolio. And if you are already in your Third Act, you may want to consider this as kind of a fun opportunity to do something that you've never done. Try small, unusual investments. Create a new hobby. Start producing something just to have fun with it, gamifying your investing to make it even more fun. And who knows? You may make a lot of money in these businesses.

Dorie Clark: "If you plan with a longer horizon than everyone else, and you're willing to endure the ups and downs along the way, you'll be able to accomplish far more than others — or even you — imagined."

---

5   Thomas Stanley and William Danko, the authors of *The Millionaire Next Door*, say it takes 22 years for most millionaires to make their first million from the time they become serious about their financial lives.

Robert Vlach (author of *The Freelance Way*): "I should have started investing 10 years earlier in my mid-20s. Bummer."

Have the moment of retirement well-calculated. Early retirement is not worth it (unless you have it well calculated and have taken other security measures). Working longer can well pay off. You need to calculate it well. Contact an expert or me if you want help with the calculation. (It is generally not publicly available in most countries. I had to work it out.)

There may be an exception to the previous statement about early retirement, which is when people purposefully earn a lot and retire very early (so-called FIRE trends = Financial Independence & Retire Early). One of the key principles here is the "four percent rule." They say anyone who retires at an early age should have enough money to make ends meet every year with an amount of four percent of their total savings or investments. (142). I'm not sure if this holds any more in today's world.

Have a good health insurance policy (in many countries it is obligatory). Establish a **risk-only** (I mean non-investment) **accident insurance policy** in time. It is a kind of protection for serious injuries. **Insure your property.** Find a good independent insurance agent/consultant.

It is said that above a certain level of savings and investments, the contribution to happiness is no longer big. The very rich are not necessarily more or less happy than the upper middle class. In my opinion, however, it is **necessary to have reserves** nowadays for health problems and aid tools, social services, and other unexpected events: health, helping children, changes in the economic or ecological environment, pandemic, relocation, etc.

Society of Actuaries View of Retirement Risks

- Longevity Risk
- Inflation Risk
- Interest Rate Risk
- Stock Market Risk
- Business Risks
- Employment Risk
- Public Policy Risks

- Unexpected Health Care Needs & Costs
- Lack of Available Facilities or Caregivers
- Loss of Ability to Live Independently
- Change in Housing Needs
- Death of a Spouse
- Other Change in Marital Status
- Unforeseen Needs of Family Members
- Bad Advice, Fraud or Theft

Source: www.soa.org/files/pd/post-retirement-charts.pdf

Three Action Steps for Building the Basics

☐ **First**: Make clear for yourself: **When do you want to retire?** Do you want to calculate the cost to retire early? Do you want to calculate how long it pays off to work?
Add the relevant tasks to your list of goals.

☐ **Second: Prepare your estimated future monthly retirement expenses.** You may want to download and use my template Prepare your estimated future monthly retirement expenses.xlsx .

There are many surveys available on what amount of monthly spending people think will suffice and what you would have to save. In the end, **it is up to you, not me or anyone else, to decide what amount and when you are financially ready.** A good rule of thumb for retirement is you should have about 75% of your pre-retirement income each year to live on. You may consider setting a nest egg goal of 15x your income for retirement.

Do you believe it is possible? Has anyone succeeded? Definitely yes, so it is possible. **Believe that this is possible for you as well.** If you haven't achieved it yet, you need to change something. There is something you don't know or can change. Find out what it is. Learn it. Change is an opportunity, and today's world is full of change. You have to want it, and you have to learn something. Success can also be learned. And if you think education is expensive, try ignoring it. Do you think it will help more? Learn from your experience or from other people. It will be faster because they have already made the mistakes.

There is a lot of research on the replacement ratio needed (what percentage of your former salary you will need in retirement). Some claim 70%, others 105%. However, none of the numbers will suit everyone. I believe it is far better to estimate your future requirements, which we will do in the following action steps.

I believe the survey that states: **satisfaction is positively related to the number of years individuals save for retirement (the longer, the higher satisfaction).** (143)

☐ **Third: Estimate your state/social security benefits and pension** both for you and your spouse. If you are a few years before retirement, you can have it calculated by a professional. Otherwise, it can be assumed that you will have something between the minimum and 2-3 times more (if you did not earn very much). You may want to check for your country. Add your employer's retirement plan income, Individual Retirement Accounts, annuities, business interests you could liquidate for income, investment income, and any other potential income.

Many households do not have a family budget at all. They don't even know how much they are spending now let alone in decades to come. How is the overall balance for you? **Do you need a more detailed plan for creating financial security?** Do you need to consult an expert or someone who has already done so? Or do you need to find something on the internet for that? Add it to your list of tasks.

Five Action Steps for Planting Your Wealth Tree

☐ Action step 1: **Think about suitable housing**. I hope you will have your mortgage paid off before retiring. Where will you live? With whom? Do you need a garden? Accessibility? Do you imagine a town, village, or cottage in the mountains? Think about transport accessibility, the distance to relatives and friends, availability of shopping, restaurants, and doctors. What's the culture like? What kind of lifestyle and activities will you enjoy? How much will it cost per month? People often forget how important all that is.

Or do you want to sell your property at a late age with the right to live there and pay for all-day care with the money earned? In that case, what will your children do when they find out they will not inherit the property?

Or do you want to sell your property and live in a mobile home? Maybe you have children across the country that you can stay with at their homes.

Or do you want to consider moving to another country? In that case, consider all the circumstances and your priorities. For example, you can get some guidance and inspiration here: https://internationalliving.com/. It is aimed at U.S. citizens, and it also includes countries from all over the world, with some European countries ranking high. It uses a lot of criteria and experiences from a large number of people. I will have another chapter on this topic later.

I once met an older couple from Australia in a campground on my trip to Zion canyon. They told me they have a camper van in the U.S., another one in Germany, and a third one in Australia. They take turns between continents based on the weather and their mood.

What do you need to do to have such suitable housing for you in time? **Add it to your tasks.**

☐ Action step 2: **Think about a suitable retirement mobility solution.**

You will not have to commute to work anymore, but transport still will be needed. Will you use public transportation, car, or another solution? How much will it cost per month? What do you need to do to achieve that state? Add it to your tasks and prioritize them.

☐ Action step 3: To what extent do you want to contribute to the **financial security of your children**? Don't forget about taxes, some of which you will still have to pay.

☐ Action step 4: Return to your written goals. Complete them to reflect what your ideal **retirement financial situation** looks like.

Are these goals PEVS (Positive, Exciting and Emotional, Visualized, and a little Scary)? Adjust them if necessary.

a)   What kind of expert help or other help do you need to achieve it?
b)   Which one knowledge/skill, if you master it and use it excellently, would have the greatest positive impact on fulfilling your financial security plan?
c)   What will you do to acquire this knowledge or ability?
d)   Take the first, albeit small, step immediately.
e)   Add to your calendar weekly reminders on this task.
f)   Always ask: which one activity would add the most value to this goal?

Repeat steps a) to f) for your **suitable housing solution.**
Then for your **retirement transport solution.**
Then for **securing your children**.

☐ Action step 5: **Do you want to be a (full-time) employee for all your life?**

Should you want to consider whether you prefer to work as an entrepreneur (with a trade license or Ltd. company), the overall effective tax rate for a sole trader is around 22% in my country. For an employee, it's around 48% in my country. Please check with a tax advisor in your country. As an entrepreneur, you can purposefully invest the extra money for many years directly into your Third Act with the help of a professional, rather than through the government. I have lived it and verified it. This is what helped me become a happy rentier.

Do you want to **increase your qualifications** (proactively or even under the pressure of circumstances)? Would you consider the possibility of **becoming a freelancer, contractor, interim manager, or working part-time**? This could help you optimize your taxes, save regularly, and invest in retirement. And what about trying out **pre-retirements** (working on projects while trying out the life of a pensioner/rentier) or starting a new business? You can get advice or coaching on all of this, including tax impacts in your country of tax residence. Train the emotional stresses associated with it. Experience what it's like to be home alone or with your family. Switch to working from home. (Many of us have tried this experience during the pandemic.)

You may want to repeat this consideration in your Third Act of life. Do what you want (work full- or part-time or start a new business), get another stream of income on monthly basis, and spend it (not having to touch your investments) or invest it (into a financial product or your health).

It's about balancing enjoyment and experiences now and postponing some of your enjoyment in favor of the future.

Trading (some of) **the present convenience for a better future life.**

Commitment over convenience.

The Relationship Between Money and Happiness

Money doesn't make you happy, but it does calm you down. And it makes you more prepared for hard times.

Many people are looking to financial security and a lot of nice possessions to make them happy in retirement. They do not know exactly what they want from life, and they are sure money will provide it for them. They believe they'll be much happier with more money... The truth is: **Money is an**

important element for survival, comfort, and enjoyment, and a tool to accomplish some life goals. It can help maintain your health and provide quality health care and healthy food. But money alone will not guarantee true happiness. That comes from self-respect, accomplishment, and satisfaction. Money cannot buy creative fulfilment. Happiness cannot be bought. **Money may get us to a neutral state, but more money cannot get us beyond that state. Happiness comes from within.** (13)

Dan Kopf says that incomes above $105,000 in the US are not associated with greater happiness. The technical term for this cut-off is the income "satiation point." (61)

According to Sarah Todd, having enough money to satisfy needs like food and shelter and achieve basic financial security makes an enormous difference in people's happiness. After those basic needs have been met, money can also boost happiness by helping us to reach our bigger aspirations. Achieving the life of our wildest dreams wouldn't require the kinds of sums the richest people in the world have accumulated. Instead, most people aspire to be "comfortable but not extravagant." (60)

Darius Foroux: What would you do if you were rich?

> Someone: "What would you do if you made a million bucks a year?"
> You: "I would probably buy a new house."
> Someone: "And then what?"
> You: "Go on a vacation."
> Someone: "And then what?"
> You: "Buy something for my partner and family."
> Someone: "And then what?"
> You: "Finally pursue my passion project!"
> Someone: "And then what?"
> You: "Um… Other than that, probably do the same things I'm doing now?" (111)

When we have more money, we think about spending it first. And then we always come back to the usual: living life. We primarily want to get rich so we can spend it on things. Some people might spend it on travel, others on luxury. But once you're done spending, you still have to do what all other happy people do: wake up, spend your day in a meaningful way, and enjoy yourself.

Even if one has a lot of money, they must know how to make it to bring them satisfaction. Based on many studies and experiments, it is enough to follow four rules:

1. **Spend money on experiences instead of things** because people return to them more often in their thoughts. This is because they are usually **shared with other people**, and social relationships greatly increase the happiness of individuals.
2. It's good to **spend money on other people**: gift-giving flushes out happiness hormones.
3. **Instead of one big spend, do several small ones at a time.** It is not so important for happiness how big a pleasure one has, but how often one **experiences small pleasures** (economic concept of the law of diminishing returns).
4. **Postpone consumption for later but pay for it now.** If we have to pay for something that no longer makes us happy, it not only does not increase the level of perceived happiness, it decreases it. Delayed-pay purchases, as evidenced by literature, lead to irresponsible decisions and debt, which further negatively affect levels of perceived happiness. (38)

The New Map of Life

According to the Stanford Center of Longevity, by the middle of this century, living to the age of 100 will become commonplace. This is more increase in a single century than across all prior millennia of human evolution combined. (Longevity is brought about by reductions in infant mortality, advances in sanitation and medicine, public education, and rising standards of living. Despite the grievous toll of the COVID-19 pandemic, the trajectory will continue its rise during the current century as well.) (58)

The conventional life course is a one-way road through scripted stages (acts of life): education, work, and retirement. In the New Map of Life, multiple life transitions are a necessity. It offers multiple routes, connecting the roles, opportunities, and obligations that 100-year lives will bring. They may be learning (including informal and lifelong, upskilling, reskilling), working (more than one primary career), caregiving, enjoying leisure, volunteering and mentoring, returning to work, launching an encore career or a new business, downsizing a home, or getting back into the game after illness or injury with physical limitations. They'll have intergenerational partnerships, which will improve the flow of knowledge, support, and care in all directions. **Flexibility is the mantra**, and course corrections are the norm and are worthy of social acceptance, even celebration. (58)

There's a high probability of living to the age of 100. **For some people, multiple transitions will be a necessity to be financially secure and healthy in retirement. They may actually experience more acts of life than just three.**

Your Financial Strategy for Watering the Wealth Tree

Henry David Thoreau: "It is better to live rich than to die rich."

One possible strategy is to enjoy all your money before you die. (13)

It's a difficult but necessary mindset shift to retire and learn it's ok now to decumulate. In fact, it's what you've been working your whole life toward. This feels counterintuitive, but unless you make this mindset shift, you will constantly struggle attempting to keep accumulating while being in the position of needing to use what you've saved.

Saving for retirement is smart. When you are retired, however, and have a good retirement income guaranteed for the rest of your life, increasing your assets while sacrificing your enjoyment is not a good way for a prosperous person to live. Wealth is having money; prosperity is enjoying it. Financial longevity is important until the day you die. It is not necessarily true that you have to leave money for your adult children. They can take care of themselves. You have planned and saved for retirement years, so spending savings seems to be a sound way in which to fund your lifestyle. **A good approach is to have a good balance between how much money you are spending and enjoying today and what you have in reserve to carry you through to the end.** (13)

Sandra Block: "Leaving a lot of money to your heirs does not guarantee tears at your funeral."

Another possible strategy may be Bill Perkins's "die with zero" approach. (33) You may want to **look at your life as the sum of your experiences**. Spending on experiences makes us happier than spending on things, and experiences don't even have to cost much. Moreover, **the value of experiences increases with time**. (Bill Perkins calls this the "dividend of memories.") Collect experiences and memories as soon as possible.

Happiness from experiences grows with time; happiness from buying things decreases with time. (159)

The main message I see there is the **goal of this strategy is to maximize the total experiences in life, not maximize financial wealth**. You would ideally die with zero in your bank account. Money is a tool, not the ultimate goal. **Think about how you will use your money to live the fullest life possible** in the time and life energy you have left. This idea from Bill Perkins is very new and good (but counterintuitive for many people).

The first objection you may have is that you must **remember your children** with your money. Bill suggests this answer: **Be intentional about how much you want to give them; the rest is yours** to maximize your experience. And **give the money to your children much earlier, when it will help them the most**. Make up your mind with this. You can give it to them right away or set up a trust/foundation for their benefit with defined terms of withdrawal. Check if your country has good legislature.[6]

---

6   In the U.S., the trust-friendly state is Wyoming; in Europe, it is in Jersey, Lichtenstein, Switzerland, Luxemburg, the Czech Republic, and Austria; in Asia it is New Zealand and some of UAE.

I share the opinion (supported by many lawyers and other experts) that **a will is not a good solution**, both because it's too random (you don't know when you will die, and it is highly probable it will have suboptimal benefit to the heirs' quality of life at that time) and has low flexibility. Have **a will just in case you die suddenly**, but a much better solution is a trust (especially if it has sound support in the law system of your country, which is not true in many countries, unfortunately).

As far as the balance between enjoying now and saving for the future goes, keep in mind that **the ability to get experiences for your money diminishes with age**. (33) Even if you take care of yourself, **your physical health will gradually deteriorate** (limiting your options and abilities to travel and play sports and also narrowing your interests and creativity). The utility of your money decreases with age. **It is clever to adjust the spending/saving ratio to your age, health, and life situation.**

Bill identifies **three variables that are critical** to maximizing your life experiences: **money, leisure, and health**. (33) They usually are **not all available at the same time**. You may find in your second act you have a good combination of money and health. But at any age, **you can maximize life experiences by balancing these three variables**. You may consider buying more health or leisure time (e.g., hiring a laundry service or house cleaning professional). And since health is the most important factor (the multiplier), you should **start investing in your health sooner rather than later,** before it's too late. **Every small investment of money and time in health will expand your experience opportunities later**.

Also, **think which experiences you should treat yourself to now because later on** you may not be able to do them (**the window of opportunity will close forever**, or the risk/benefit ratio will increase too much). You can also plan experiences (activities or events) for the rest of your life. Write down your dreams (don't worry about money now), and then assign them to future life periods. **It's not a "bucket list." It's proactive planning.**

Now you might be wondering… *How should I prioritize experiences for my money?* One of the answers is **consider investing money first in experiences that bring long-lasting memories**. Don't put these off until it's too late. Also, **acknowledge that at some point in time, your wealth will be at its highest and may not grow any further**. From this time, **start withdrawing more than saving**. This will allow you the maximum experience. From the simulations that have been done, the peak point seems to be somewhere between 45 and 60 years (even more for very healthy people). (33). From here, you **stop having the overall goal of maximizing your finances**. (You still can consider part-time work, phased retirement, or occasional projects.)

Do the calculations on the savings needed to survive for the rest of your life (plus investing in your health and some reserves), or have it done for you. This will give you the peace of mind to increase your spending. Even so, it won't be an easy **step**, but it **is necessary if you want to get the most out of your Third Act of life.** Occasionally review your list of experiences in the remaining part of your Third Act.

I agree with Bill to **be bold in your choice of experiences even at an older age, realistically weighing the risks** you can accept. (Don't irrationally think of only the worst scenario as your inner saboteurs tell you). **Also, think about the risk of missing out on opportunities for better life experiences.** Let the sage within you choose. After all, **the purpose of life is to collect memories**.

☐ **Action step:** Go back to your list of goals and review your goals in terms of your financial plan and experiences.

You have your financial plan ready. Stick to it, or adjust to changing conditions, and look forward to retiring financially secure, where you'll do almost anything you want, when you want, with whom you want, wherever you want, for as long as you want. **Enjoy your wealthy Third Act of life — when the time comes.** Your retirement years will be the best time of your life.

Visit **www.livingyourbestthirdact.com**. There you will find free templates, exercises, checklists, outlines, worksheets, and physical action plans.

THIRD ACT
RESOURCES

Chapter 6: Your Health Plan For Retirement: Body Care & Physical Health

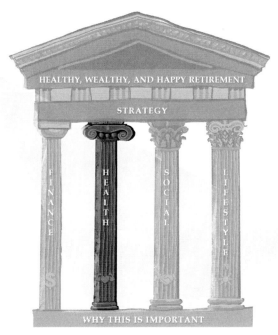

> "To prevent diseases, you don't have to make big life-style changes; to reverse diseases, much bigger changes are needed. You can make the changes at any age." Dean Ornish

Your health in retirement (both physical and mental) will depend on how you take care of it — during all of your life. If you do not actively take care, it will deteriorate over time.

Your mission for this chapter — should you choose to accept it — is to do your best to keep your health as good as possible. Imagine retiring with optimal health and being able to do almost anything you want in retirement. The decades of your retirement will be a joy to look forward to and experience fully.

In this chapter, we will discuss the Health Plan for Retirement Preparation: Body Care & Physical Health. The importance of health increases with age. If you are healthy, you can do almost anything you want. Without good health, you can never be truly rich.

Read this chapter to see:
— The four distinct steps of the "health equation"
— How to understand the context of retirement health planning
— Some of the biggest food lies causing suffering for billions of people
— What affects life longevity according to scientific research
— What the "blue zones" are
— How to build your health plan
— The main health areas to avoid
— Basics of diet and weight loss
— The biggest obstacles in implementing food choices you already know
— Why do you eat? How do you eat? What do you eat? When do you eat?
— Easy to implement breakthroughs for a healthier life
— The relationship between the immune system and the gut
— The recommended minimum steps approach
— The latest knowledge on Alzheimer prevention
— Microbiota in old age
— Practical recommendations
— 19-step system to create your Health Plan

You may be thinking: *is this another book telling me I have to give up my favorite stuff? Eat a more plant-based diet?* I don't prefer that. *Why do I need to worry about my health now? My health is predetermined by my genetics, so why should I care? How can this book be beneficial to me?*

No, what I am saying is there are options for you. Now more than ever, it's important for people to look beyond their financial numbers and savings habits and focus on their health-related factors as well. Oftentimes, people think the extra time they will have in retirement will provide the motivation they need to live a healthier life compared to when they were working... but old habits are hard to break, and new habits are hard to make. Retirement only magnifies what you already are, particularly when it comes to health. If you frequent the couch, mostly watching TV, and prefer fatty foods, retirement will only provide more time to reinforce those habits. And the effects of unhealthy lifestyle choices compound very slowly, until one day... heart attack, stroke, cancer, out-of-control blood sugar, with little to no warning.

Poor nutrition is one of the leading risk factors for chronic disease, which accounts for 70% of all deaths in the United States (116).

Dr. David Katz: "We already know all that we need to know to reduce, by 80%, the five major killers in our country. We don't need any more fancy drugs or equipment or more Nobel Prizes. We know all we need to know today."

I cannot stress enough the importance of health in the Third Act. We will see more and more people who must change their plans completely because of the impact of disease. Not being able to enjoy your Third Act is not good. Moreover, health is a big part of relationships and has an impact on them, whether with your spouse, family, friends, or community. For instance, in a couple where only one out of the two is committed to their health, one could become sick, and then the other one becomes their caregiver.

Also, health has a direct impact on the lifestyle you can have, emotional status, travel possibilities, and overall happiness.

This chapter is about how creating a healthy lifestyle now allows you to reap the benefits during retirement. Instead of suffering during this time, as too many people are, you can have a Third Act that truly celebrates your life.

What should I be concerned about planning for my health in my Third Act preparation?

Planning for your health includes many factors. You may think: this health system is too complicated. To make this complex discipline clearer, I have structured it into four distinct steps I call the "health equation":

1)   Understanding the context
2)   Building the basics
3)   Planting your health tree
4)   Watering your health tree

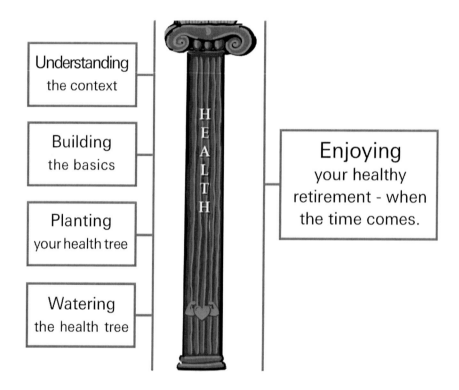

In understanding the context, you will see why we are sicker than ever, the biggest food lies, what affects life longevity, neglecting our health risks, why we must take special care of ourselves and appreciate our health before it is lost, and conclusions from so-called blue zones.

In building the preparation basics, you will learn main health areas to avoid, some facts on diet and weight loss, the biggest obstacles in implementing food choices (that you already know), why you eat, how you eat, and what you eat. You will read 10 easy to implement breakthroughs, information about the immune system and healthy gut relationship, recommended minimum steps, dieting principles, recent knowledge about carbs, top 12 best foods to reduce inflammation, recent knowledge about protein consumption, probiotics, flatulence, food intolerance and lactose, genomic sequencing, and microbiota in old age.

Planting your health tree will show you practical recommendations.

Watering the health tree will provide you with 18 action steps to create your retirement health plan.

By implementing these four health equation steps, you will be prepared to retire healthy and do almost anything you want in your Third Act.

Ralph Marston, a former professional football player: "There are plenty of difficult obstacles in your path. Don't allow yourself to become one of them."

Understanding the Context

You may wonder what is different about preparing your health plan for the Third Act compared to the normal daily care of your health you can read about elsewhere. Let me explain the context.

Life-span versus health-span ("health longevity") is a broadly discussed concept recently. Our health-spans don't match our life-spans. We are the most obese, the most stressed, the least satisfied, and the most addicted in modern human history. For the first time in history, children will live shorter lives than their parents. Dr. Michael Greger: "The reason our kids will most likely live shorter lives than us is because of the obesity epidemic."

Although most people agree that having good physical and mental health is essential to achieving optimal well-being, we have major health challenges. In the United States, 80% of Americans aged 65 and older have a chronic condition, 68% have more than two conditions, and 42% live with a disability. (86)

The Stanford Center on Longevity says that while median life expectancies have increased dramatically over the past century, the years in which people are healthy, mobile, mentally sharp, and free of pain (defined as health-span) have not kept pace. (43) Healthy aging requires investments in health at every life stage.

According to the U.S. Burden of Disease Collaborators in 2018, the gap between our total life expectancy and our healthy life expectancy, defined as the years lived in full health and free of disability, is 12.4 years in the U.S. In Canada, it is 10.9 years, and 10.4 in Japan. (86)

The U.S. has more scientists, doctors, therapists, nutritionists, and gyms per capita now than at any other time and place in human history. Why is it that, despite massive advances in technology, medicine, and science, we're sicker than ever? (55)

Seventy percent of adults have already been diagnosed with a chronic disease. Eighty percent of the health care costs are spent on managing chronic diseases. Life expectancy continues to fall, including a 2.2 year drop since 2020.

Twenty-four percent of adults currently suffer from a mental illness or mood disorder. Forty-seven percent of adults will experience a mental illness during their lifetime. Five of the top 10 causes of death are strongly tied to emotional trauma. The hours of sleep people get per night has dropped from 7.9 in 1942 to just 6.8. The percentage of overweight and obese children has tripled since 1970. Over one third of American children are overweight or obese. Last year, there were two million new cases of cancer diagnosed. Six million Americans are now living with Alzheimer's disease. (55)

average course of life over the next decade.

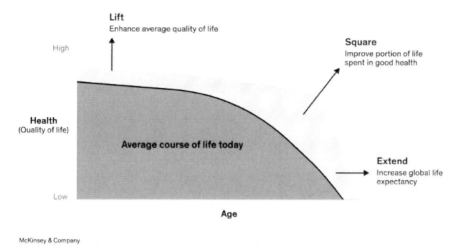

McKinsey & Company

(45)

The risks involved when we start neglecting our health are real and harder to correct as we continue to age. For many, lockdown has compounded the impact, resulting in a loss of confidence and feelings of depression. (34)

Health problems can multiply, especially if you do not take care of yourself. Feeling good about yourself at midlife and later is an important aspect of overall well-being. Also, good health is important so you do not become dependent on others, which could have a serious effect on your self-esteem and sense of freedom. We often do not appreciate our great health until it is lost. (31)

Albert Schweitzer: "Happiness? That's nothing more than health and a poor memory."

The American Heart Association states: "Science has linked being inactive and sitting too much with higher risk of heart disease, type 2 diabetes, colon and lung cancers, and early death." (59)

I have very demanding job and do not have time/energy to take care of my health. Why should I listen to you?

The majority of people in Western nations are unwilling to do as much as they can for their health. Eighty percent of people worldwide do not do regular active physical activity. Seventy percent of people sleep less than eight hours a day. About 300,000 Americans die prematurely each year because of physical inactivity and poor diet (second to smoking, which kills 400,000). WHO: nearly 18 million people die from heart disease every year. (31)

Retirement allows you more opportunity to spend time on your health. You can exercise your right to retire healthier and happier. WHO definition: "Health is a state of complete physical, mental, and social well-being, and not merely the absence of disease or infirmity." (145)

Illness, such as cancer, is a wake-up call. It's an opportunity to re-evaluate your life from a new perspective and decide if the life you have been living is the life you want to continue living, or if you're ready to step up to a higher quality, happier, healthier, more fulfilling life that you truly deserve. (59)

According to a "Metabolic Syndrome and Related Disorders" study, one in eight adults have optimal metabolic health, which means over 87% of us have an elevated risk of diseases related to poor metabolism. (42)

I have good genes. Do I need to take any special measures?

One of many excuses is that you cannot fight genetics. But genetically based aging aspects are much less prominent than people think. A MacArthur Foundation study showed that only 30% of how we age can be attributed to genes. Seventy percent is determined by our lifestyle choices. Newer sources even say that genes account for less than 7% of the life-span, so health and life longevity are more than 90% in our hands. **Successful aging is mostly within our control.** Stop making excuses about your genes. (31) (100)

If a particular disease-oriented gene doesn't express itself, nothing happens. It is really about gene expression rather than the existence of the gene itself. We do have influence over gene expression through our lifestyle. (Epigenetics) (88). Health and quality old age are a matter of choices and priorities.

Some may think: I am regularly visiting my doctor(s), why should I know more?

You must take special care of yourself as no one else will. You are responsible for your health. Your doctors, your hospital, your health insurance policy... none of them can do even one hundredth as much as you can. Become your own inner healer. Your three best doctors will always be exercise, wholesome food, and a positive attitude.

We don't have a health care system. We have a disease-care system. It deals with fixing what is broken, not maintaining good health. It is reactive, not proactive. (88)

Has your primary care physician asked you about your diet, exercise plan, social relationships, or level of stress? Did they offer any unsolicited advice in any of those areas? Probably not. This could be because it isn't their specialty, they are overloaded, or the system has little to no incentive in prevention. Their education probably didn't include any extensive training on these topics.

Even though there are thousands of peer-reviewed studies in scientific literature discussing the impact of diet, environment, and lifestyle on cancer and other metabolically related diseases like heart disease and diabetes, most conventional medical doctors and oncologists are unfortunately not trained more than a few hours in nutrition and lifestyle. (59)

I would like to add a macroeconomic view, too: If there was more emphasis on prevention, it would eventually decrease the financial load on the health care system, and healthier people would work longer and increase tax collection.

Are you getting fitter or fatter?

Nathan Crane: "We are always either healing, and moving toward health, or we are deteriorating, and moving toward disease. Healing is the process. Health is the outcome. It's a lifestyle. And it's a way of being, a way of thinking, and a way of living." (59)

Please understand, I don't have all of the answers for you. Please listen, read, learn from real experts (not social media "gurus"), question everything with an open mind, research on your own, and find your own answers and solutions.

If you are ill, be patient. It took a long time to get sick, it's going to take time to heal.

Baseball legend Satchel Paige: "How old would you be if you didn't know how old you were?"

Peter Attia: "Going from zero weekly exercise to just ninety minutes per week can reduce your risk of dying from all causes by 14 percent. It's very hard to find a drug that can do that." (156)

This book is an opportunity for you to focus on the health part of your life now (whatever act of life you are in), especially if you did not focus on it before.

Dr. Tom O'Bryan: "Allocate one hour a week to learn more, to focus on you and your family health." (Come back to this or another book, watch webinars, etc.) "Change the paradigm, the lifestyle you live. It takes months."

The Biggest Food Lies Causing Suffering for Billions of People

#1: **Healthy eating is confusing and complicated.** Actually, nutritional truth is not that controversial. You can reduce the risk of chronic diseases by more than 80% by doing four simple things: eating a healthful diet (more on this later), not smoking, having a healthy weight, and regularly exercising.

#2: **It can't be real if my doctor doesn't know it.** Most doctors do not know much about the influence of nutrition, poor diet, and lifestyle on prevention and recovery, or they do not discuss this with their patients for different reasons.

#3: **Healthy food is boring.** The truth is: Good-for-you foods, both for the short-term and long-term, are not opposite to fun-for-you ones. (39) And also, real, whole, fresh, plant-based food can be easy to prepare.

Our diet is killing us, and the way we produce our food is killing our planet. Each individual decision matters. And sometimes people change their diet because it's helping both the world and their health.

Don't have the "Jim Fixx mindset." Jim Fixx was a world-renown long-distance runner who staunchly maintained that diet is irrelevant as long as you keep your exercise levels high. He "grandstanded" his position by living on a diet very heavy in cheeseburgers. He died roadside in the middle of a solitary run due to a massive heart attack. His autopsy revealed highly occluded arteries. (88)

What Affects Life Longevity According to Scientific Research?

— Close and good personal relationships and interactions.
— Social connections (family, friends, communities). The number does not matter as much as quality. Loneliness kills.
— Having a loved one I can count on improves physical and mental health.
— Wanting quick satisfaction at the expense of relationships shortens life. Maintaining good long-term relationships is an art.
— Actively work to replace retired colleagues with playmates. (1)

E. Blackburn, Nobelist, stated aging = telomere shortening.[7] Telomere shortening was found to be caused by long-term stress. The length of telomeres is not only determined by age. Living conditions, and **our responses to them**, really affect life expectancy. And we have more control over that than we think. Life attitude is important. Children living in an environment of war, violence, and racism have shorter telomeres. On the contrary, life in tightly bound communities,

---

7   Telomeres are the terminal parts of chromosomes. Gradual shortening of telomere length leads to cell aging and programmed cell death.

long and happy marriages, and lifelong friendships improve telomere maintenance. Thus, where we live affects the length of the telomere. (144)

Dan Buettner of *National Geographic* says life expectancy is given by 10% of genes. The rest is determined by lifestyle (study of Danish twins). But what exactly does that mean? First, the probability of surviving 100 years is not great, even if you try hard (in the US now it's only one in 5,000 people). We are programmed for "procreative success" — raising children and grandchildren. Good lifestyle is not enough to live to 100. You would have to inherit good genetics here. But according to science, the ability of the human body is to live 90 years in good health. Some say normal human life-span is between 96 and 106 years. The life expectancy in the U.S. in 2018 was 78.7 years (76.2 for men, 81.2 for women), and it's predicted to rise to 85 by 2050. In the UK in 2019, it was 79.4 years for males and 83.1 years for females. (51, 86) So **we are playing for about 8 to 14 years of a healthy life.**

You may have heard of so-called **blue zones**. The five blue zones of the world are Okinawa, Japan; Sardinia (Nuoro), Italy; Nicoya, Costa Rica; Ikaria, Greece; and Loma Linda, California. These are places where people live the longest and healthiest lives. A study of these zones concluded:
— First, a little heresy: old people do not physically exercise in these blue zones (in the traditional sense).
— People in these zones have their environment set up in such a way that it forces them to move around daily: stairs; trips to the shop, friends, or church; they cook by hand, walk, and work in the garden. They enjoy the motion.
— They know how to slow down (prayer, honor the feasts, etc.) at least 15 minutes a day. They know how to reduce stress and laugh more and prioritize good sleep.
— They have a vocabulary for the meaning of life, such as *ikigai*[8] in Okinawa or *plan de vida* in Nicaragua — the reason

---

8   Japanese concept of longevity from the island of Okinawa; means a reason to get up in the morning, a strong sense of purpose in life, or a personal vision.

to get out of bed in the morning. The most dangerous years of life are after birth (infant mortality) and then after retirement. People in blue zones have the right mindset — they know their purpose. Anyone who purposefully knows their meaning and brings it to life adds about 7 years to his life.

— People from the blue zones mainly eat vegetables, little meat (mostly fish), a lot of legumes, and nuts. They don't overeat. They can get up from the table in time (*Hara Hachi Bu*[9]), avoid processed foods, eat nutrient -dense foods, and practice time-restricted feeding. Food is culture and wisdom.

— They have social lives, live in a healthy community, are interconnected, and have relationships with family, children, and aging parents. They mostly live in a community based on faith, which adds 4 to 14 years with weekly participation. And they live in the right "tribe or parentage" — either born there or proactively surrounded by the right people. The community believes that it's good to be old. (1, 85)

You can create your own "blue zone" around you any-where you are now.

A Framingham study showed if three of your close friends are obese, there is a 50% probability you will be, too. Surround yourself with friends who do physical activity, ride a bike, garden, drink little, eat well, are active, and are trustworthy. There is no long-term miracle diet. (No diet in history has worked for more than 2% of the population.) There is no quick pill or anything like that for longevity.

Openness, generosity, positive attitude toward other people, optimism (both about the future and about one's illnesses) can't be ordered, but it can be worked on (for example with the help of a coach, mentor, books, or self-education). Rejoice in the little things. And have deep interests. (4)

You may be asking about the impact of COVID-19. We don't yet know the long-lasting effects on our health-spans and

9   Hara Hachi Bu: Enjoy Food and Lose Weight With This Simple Japanese Phrase (https://www.bluezones.com/2017/12/hara-hachi-bu-enjoy-food-and-lose-weight-with-this-simple-phrase/#)

life-spans, but we know that in 2020, it shaved off more than one year of average life expectancy in the United States. (68)

☐ **Health goal action step**
☐ How would your health be different if it was perfect in every way?
☐ What do you not want to significantly worsen until retirement? Or what do you want to significantly improve? Add it to your list of goals now.

Mickey Mantle: "If I knew I was going to live so long, I'd have taken better care of myself."

My friend Jim has a friend, and her dad had a heart attack at 60 years old. It forced him to go on disability, and then he retired at 65. He lived to 86 years old, and basically all he did those 26 years was sit in a chair and watch TV all day. That was how he lived his Third Act. Pretty sad story. It is better to start taking care of yourself as soon as possible. And it is never too late.

Norman Vincent Peale: "Start where you are. Don't wait for someone else to change things for you. Do it yourself."

Bonnie Prudden: "You can't turn back the clock. But you can wind it up again."

Building the Basics

This is the second part of the health equation.

You may want to download the checklist for this chapter from **www.livingyourbestthirdact.com**: Health plan checklist.pdf.

Building The Basics: Main Areas to Avoid

Pay attention to **early prevention** of at least **the greatest risks:** cardiovascular disease, cancer (prostate, lung, colon, etc.), diabetes mellitus, obesity, COVID, stroke, and dementia. You have probably heard it many times, but I have to say it again: Don't smoke, watch your blood pressure,[10] watch your cholesterol and your kidneys (creatinine), do not abuse alcohol, and watch your weight. I will say more on how to fight obesity in a moment. These basic measures will halve the risk of a stroke (3rd most common cause of death). (145)

Gautam Buddha: "The trouble is, you think you have time."

The #1 killer in our society isn't heart disease, cancer, diabetes, stroke, or dementia. It is health care illiteracy. Every one of the abovementioned largest risks is subject to intervention. It means they are heavily influenced by the lifestyle choices that we make. (88)

Building The Basics: Diet and Weight Loss

Dr. Mark Hyman: "Eleven million people per year die from eating the wrong foods in the U.S. Food is the number one killer today. Even before COVID, we saw life expectancy start to go down in the U.S."

Forty-eight percent of Canadians are overweight, 13% obese. Over two-thirds of adult Americans are overweight or obese, and nearly 40% of adult Americans are obese. The average American today weighs 15 pounds more than 20 years ago — and they haven't gotten any taller. (56, 88)

The costs that obese people impose on the health system are already enormous. In the United States, they amount to 173 billion USD per year. Moreover, according to the available forecasts, the number of obese people is set to rise, and so will the number of diabetics. According to the World Health Organization, almost half of the U.S. adult population could be obese by 2030, and up to a billion people worldwide could be directly obese. (135).

Fully one-third of the U.S. population (84 million) are pre-diabetic and don't know it. The prevalence of obesity in children has increased markedly. Obesity has also been increasing rapidly throughout the world, and the incidence of obesity nearly

---

10 High blood pressure is a silent killer, as many people who suffer from hypertension are totally unaware. WHO estimates that close to half the people who have dangerously high blood pressure don't know it. But you have a lot of control over your blood pressure through your lifestyle.

doubled from 1991 to 1998. Obesity has been declared by WHO a worldwide epidemic. That speaks clearly to our lack of health care literacy. But it can be avoided. Although only 10-20% of the population manage to maintain the same weight, it can be done. Gaining weight with age is avoidable. It is a matter of being committed to remaining healthy instead of eating more than one must. It requires a commitment to some study plus a willingness to rid your lifestyle of bad practices. (56, 88)

Any dietary adjustment only makes sense if you follow it for a long time and feel good thanks to it for many years.

Planning out a week's worth of healthy, fresh meals will help you steer away from those post-work takeaways. If you're working from home, a planned recipe and ingredients in the fridge also helps you shut down the laptop and switch into home mode.

You are what you eat! How many times have you heard that over the years? But do you really know what it means? What impact does your nutrition have on your gut, microbiome, and genetic expression?

The root cause of disease is: "Poor lifestyle, poor environment, toxic food air and water, the accumulation of chemicals and toxins in the system, with the accumulation of stress, unhappiness, anger, fear..." (53)

Dr. Mark Hyman: "Our food system, from end to end, is both the cause and the cure for most of the health problems that we're facing today in the world."

Dr. Jolene Brighten: "Food is not just about the nutrients. Food is also information (about our environment)."

Biggest Obstacles in Implementing Food Choices You Already Know

The biggest obstacle is not the lack of knowledge or willpower. It is believing it takes too much time, it costs too much money, it can be confusing, social pressures make it difficult, and changing habits is hard. (39) Do you identify with any of these obstacles?

This book should help you to overcome the obstacles.

Change is difficult, especially when it comes to habits entrenched in our minds for decades. It is hard to move away from habits built on comfort and convenience. At some moment (before it is too late), you have to recognize what your lifestyle is doing to you. Change is possible in any area of our lives, given adequate knowledge and motivation.

One of the biggest obstacles that may get in the way of your success is the potential lack of support from families and friends. Remember: You can make this choice for your health, and you are not alone in this journey.

Choose your WHY. How will your life change when you meet your health goals?

I divide the topic of diet and weight loss into three parts: 1) why you eat, 2) how you eat, and 3) what you eat and when.

Why You Eat

My body knows best (through my taste) what it wants. Why shouldn't I listen to my taste?

Weight loss is about your head. If you eat too much or unhealthily, first of all, admit you have a problem. And only if you really want to solve it is it possible.

Experts agree that for most people, overeating is not from feelings of hunger but for psychological reasons (internal saboteurs). You get bored, you hate yourself, you feel bad, nervous, or unhappy, and food gives you short-term pleasure. The only sustainable diet or way out of this is to activate positive thinking. That way you won't be bored or feel unhappy, and there won't be an empty space crying out to be filled with food. Learn to increase positive thinking. It will strengthen the immune system, reduce inflammatory reactions to stressful situations, lower blood pressure and the risk of flu, improve sleep quality, and lower the likelihood of diabetes or stroke. (20)

How You Eat

Chew eat each bite consciously and attentively, paying full attention to its taste and shape, and perceive it with all your senses. Some may have to close their eyes. Each bite will bring much more pleasure. Less food will be enough to satisfy the same craving.

☐ **Action step**: Promise yourself you'll **eat mindfully** for at least one month.

What And When You Eat

If or when you decide to change your diet, the most important period will be the first six months, during which success will stabilize or not. (21) Start now even if the first step is the hardest. And discuss it with your loved ones. More on that in a moment.

I can confirm that at first you will be chased by a "sweet tooth," but soon you will not miss unhealthy food anymore.

Ask yourself these four questions from Kim Williams:
— How long do you want to live?
— How much life do you want to have in the time that you have left?
— How sick do you want to be?
— Is there any food that tastes better than your health? (112)

Every time you eat, you may want to look at food like this: Is this food going to strengthen me or weaken me?

Customize your daily food intake to your circadian rhythm (the bodily perception of time). Breakfast like a king, lunch like a prince, and dine like a peasant. Eliminate snacks. (They are often just a form of boredom or discomfort.) (100)

Relationship between Your Immune System and Your Gut

You may be thinking: *I am exercising and not eating much but still gaining weight. What should I do?*

Twenty-five hundred years ago, Hippocrates stated, "All disease begins in the gut."

Improper diet causes diseases. You probably know that. This applies not only to excess weight but also to possible chronic diseases. (21)

But not everyone has sufficient awareness of the details and internal context. Let's see what current science has to say about this. This field is one of the most researched now. If you are inclined as I used to be (much to my detriment) to call it nonsense, try to wait at least until the end of this chapter to make your condemnations.

Immune system and healthy gut challenge. Proper diet can influence the adult microbiome: Bacteria hold genes and use many energy sources and "switch on" those most effective in a given situation.

In the book *10% Human: How Your Body's Microbes Hold the Key to Health and Happiness*, Alanna Collen (22) claims we are only ten percent "human." For each of the cells that make up your body, there are nine "stowaways," bacteria and fungal organisms, etc. (21) An adult carries about one kilogram of bacteria in their gut. And these multiply and change rapidly. (22) The microbes you host in your body during your lifetime together weigh as much as five African elephants. You are not an individual but a colony. This microbiome (or microflora, all microorganisms found in our bodies and their genomes) contains 100,000 times more genes than the human genome, so we can shape 99% of our genetic material to benefit our health.

While we used to think that microbes didn't matter much, new scientific findings are revealing a different story, one in which microbes control our bodies, and the road to health is not possible without them. Microbial imbalances are common in people with allergies and autoimmune diseases. Nor can you lose weight permanently without restoring the gut microbiota. (22)

About 70% of our immunity is provided by our gut. (21) As you treat your gut, so it will treat you. As long as we live in balance with our microbes (thanks to a healthy gut), everything is OK. Otherwise, there are problems. Microbial colonies affect our weight, immune system, mental health, and even our choice of partner. Much of the disease that currently plagues humanity (obesity, autism, mental illness, digestive problems, allergies, autoimmune diseases, and even cancer) are due to our failure to cultivate the relationship with our colony of microbes. But unlike our own human cells, we can change our microbes for the better.

WHO in 2022: Inflammatory chronic degenerative conditions represent the number one cause of death on our planet. (145) According to Nature Medicine journal, chronic, unresolved inflammation is the leading cause of the diseases that are most likely to shorten our lives. Inflammation accelerates the aging process ("inflammageing").

The common denominator of the seemingly unrelated diseases of the 21st century, from obesity to allergies and autoimmune diseases to mental health disorders, **is inflammation**. Our immune systems are more active than ever. We have got rid of most of the former infectious diseases. (Let's not consider COVID now. We will get rid of it, too.) But we have also lost our balance with friendly microbes. (21) Poor diet leads to permeability of the gut wall (leaky gut). Thus, harmful yeasts, parasites, viruses, fungi, and other substances can enter the blood. This begins to affect and provoke the immune system and the brain (through the vagus nerve). The result is inflammation, which causes chronic diseases. (22)

According to the latest research, even Parkinson's disease tracks back to the microbiome of the large intestine (constipation being the first symptom 2-5 years in advance). (42)

Inflammation is always correlated to a leaky gut. (42)

How do you restore a permeable gut wall? Just support the right microbes with the right diet and give them enough fiber. That means more plant food. Fiber is the largest part of the gut bacteria's food.

Increased incidence of digestive disorders is directly related to a prosperous society. (21)

The good news is we already know the importance of the microbiome and the good diet to help us live long (with full physical and mental health), and your microbiome status is within your control. Make simple changes throughout the day. (42), (51)

More good news is that it is never too late to start making dietary and lifestyle changes to support proper immune regulation.

The Recommended Minimum Steps Approach

☐ **Homework**: Take notes while reading of the steps you decide to take and what resonates with you. Then include them in your list of goals. Decide what steps you want to enter into your calendar. For some steps, you may want to place a sticky note onto your refrigerator and/or put the piece of paper with your goals and steps on your mirror to see it while you brush your teeth.

You may be wondering: *What should I do with all this?* At a minimum, remember: **Your health is determined by what you don't eat** (7). Or the foods you stop eating have a much greater impact on your health than the ones you start eating. (9)

Next: Take care of your gut bacteria. Make sure they are properly nourished, and they will provide care and nourishment for you. Eat right, even if in some cases it's a little more expensive and takes a little longer to prepare and consume (in life you get what you pay for). And also, don't go shopping with an empty stomach, or at least go with a solid shopping list, i.e., shop with your brain. (21)

Jonathan Landsman: "Pay close attention to what your gut is telling you. It's your second brain and should NOT be ignored."

Obesity and Microbiota

There is evidence that **obesity is not simply the result of a difference between calorie intake and calorie expenditure.** New discoveries have shown the impact of diet on body weight in a new light. Because of the link between diet (especially fiber), microbes, SCFAs[11], intestinal permeability, and chronic inflammation, **obesity appears to be a disease of energy regulation rather than simple overeating.** It is thought that poor diet is just one pathway to weight gain, and that anything that disrupts the microbiota (including antibiotics) can have the same effect. What matters is whether substances that are harmful get from the gut into the blood. And that brings us back to proper nutrition and getting enough fiber. (7) (22)

Although the evidence for causation in humans is not yet clear, much evidence points to the **interplay between the microbiota and the immune system as the cause of disease.** The microbes in the colon shape the immune system of the whole body. It is certain that we need to modify our diet and lifestyle habits to benefit the microbiota. (7)

Dean Ornish: "The latest research shows that even basic lifestyle habits not only greatly reduce the risk of many common diseases, and extend life expectancy an average of 12-14 years, but also reduce moderate to severe Covid problems and long Covid symptoms." (https://www.ornish.com/)

---

11 SCFAs are short-chain fatty acids formed during the fermentation process in the colon. They are a source of energy for the epithelial cells of the colon; their most important food sources are fruits, vegetables, and legumes.

What Is the Dieting Principles Blueprint? Easy to Implement Breakthroughs for a Healthier Life

There are so many recommended and popular diets and supplements. How can I orient myself in this mess?

You may want to implement some easy, powerful breakthroughs for a healthier life, as shared by Ocean and John Robbins:

— **Eat real food.** Not the ultra-processed food-like industrial substances. The food industry tries to make products as addictive as possible. (Engineered food = adding sugar, salt, fat).[12] Nature does not make bad fats, factories do. If you are not sure if the food is processed, ask yourself if your grandmother would recognize it.

— **Don't eat too much**. An average American eats 500 calories too much each day.

— **Mostly eat plants and plant-based fiber.** (Less than 5% of Americans get the recommended daily amount of fiber). Eat fresh vegetables and fruits. Eat a nutrient-rich diet.

— **Drink green tea and coffee for antioxidants**. No sugar and cream. (But some people have trouble metabolizing caffeine).

— **Eat mushrooms**. They prevent some types of cancer.

— **Eat berries**.

— **Eat beans and legumes**. Source of protein, fiber, vitamins, minerals… From research in 2004: Every 2 tablespoons daily increase was correlated to 8% reduction in risk of death.

— **Eat greens.** In a study on diet and mental function of 1,000

---

12 Food addiction is prevalent among those 50+. A new poll from the University of Michigan reveals that 1 in 8 Americans over 50 have signs of food addiction, including overwhelming cravings for sweets, salty snacks, sugary drinks, fast food, and other highly processed foods. The word addiction may seem strong when it comes to food, but research has shown that our brains respond as strongly to highly processed foods, especially those highest in sugar, simple starches, and fat, as they do to tobacco, alcohol, and other addictive substances. (133)

elderly people, those who ate green leafy vegetables once or twice a day had the cognitive functioning of someone 11 years younger.
— **Use spices.** Most have true health benefits.
— **Create your habits and they will create you back.** Implementation is about habits. Lots of people who are suffering from ill health are also facing mental fatigue, which makes it harder to make good decisions. Key to success: Create systems and norms. Move from the path of least resistance. (39)

Alex Mathers: "Processed food is bad for us and slowly makes us ill. There's no processed alternative that's any better."

What if I want to know more details?
Based on the work of Justin and Erica Sonnenburg and Alanna Collen, intensive research is being carried out in the dieting principles direction. What the literature fairly agrees on are the following principles:
— Avoid the overuse of antibiotics as much as possible (they harm beneficial microbes), including indirect intake. (Every time you take a bite of meat or an animal product or a sip of milk from a factory farm, you're getting a dose of antibiotics from animals fed with antibiotics.)
— Because washing and using deodorants also changes our skin microbiota, it is a good idea to avoid house hold chemicals (chemical and toxic cleaning and cosmetic products). Often vinegar, lemon juice, and soap are sufficient for cleaning. Do not overdo it with disinfection in everyday life.
— Eating right (a powerful and accessible tool that each of us has to program the microbes that control many aspects of our biology). (7, 22)

Most of the literature recommends:
• Whole grain, plant-based diet. Maximally diversified.
• A diet high in polysaccharides, e.g. green barley,

sprouted grain.

- Significant reduction/elimination of foods rich in animal protein and fat.
- Adequate amounts of vegetable fats.
- Olives and extra virgin olive oil
- Fatty fish: salmon, sardines, herring, mackerel, anchovies.
- Turmeric. Add a dash of black pepper and eat with healthy fats.
- Berries, such as blueberries, blackberries, raspberries, strawberries, and cranberries. Cherries.
- Avocados.
- Eat a diet with lots of green leafy vegetables and fruits (more vegetables than fruits, more than 400 grams daily) and moderate serving sizes. The idea is to get 5-8 (to 10) cups of vegetables a day (42). That is not easy to do but can be done. Spinach, kale, chard, arugula, Swiss chard, and collards. Bok choy (114). Add arugula, spinach, cabbage, water crest - contain nitrate compounds (42).
- Organic green tea. The best type is matcha green tea.
- Cruciferous vegetables. These super healthy members of the Brassica family include Brussels sprouts, broccoli, cauliflower, kale, and mustard greens.
- Coconut oil. Organic, unrefined.
- Mushrooms. (Popular are Shitake. In some countries, it is common to go into the forest and pick many kinds of edible mushrooms yourself.)
- Carminative herbs.
- Add fermented/sprouted foods (and possibly supplements) to your other foods (pickles, kimchi, sauerkraut, low-sweetened kombucha, miso, etc., fermented dairy and vegetable products). Start slowly and get your body used to it. They have much higher health benefits than the price increase. You will absorb more of it in comparison to synthetic supplements.

What is the Recent Knowledge about Carbs?

According to goodnesslover.com, you may have heard about carb danger or even about some of the no-carb diets. How do you pick the best kind of carbohydrates? Always first choose whole plant foods rich in fiber, full of vitamins and minerals, and low in added sugars and unhealthy fats, and limit simple, refined carbohydrates, including sweeteners. Choose the ones which are as close to their whole form as possible. A variety of complex carbohydrates will support diversity in your microbiome. (113)

What is the Recent Knowledge about Protein Consumption?

According to foodrevolution.org, older adults tend not to absorb protein as efficiently, nor eat as much, so as a result seniors may also need more protein. The Mayo Clinic recommends that anyone over age 65 should get between 0.44 and 0.52 grams of daily protein per pound of body weight. (This means a senior who weighs 150 pounds might need 66-78 grams of protein per day.) Most American adults eat substantially more than the recommended amount — averaging more than 100 grams of protein per day. And most Europeans get more than they need, too. (118) If you're eating enough food so you don't lose weight, and you're eating a variety of whole foods, it's almost impossible to consume too little protein.

More dieting principles:
— **Avoid yo-yo diets** or intense restrictions that you can't maintain over the long run. (42) Eat a variety.
— **Eat lots of fiber.** According to the American Heart Association, the recommended daily intake of fiber is 25 grams for adults. In some other countries, they

recommend 30 grams.

— **Eat sourdough bread** made from whole meal flour.
— **Eat fish**.
— **Polyphenols**[13] in legumes. Raw, uncooked nuts (30 grams daily) and seeds as a main source of fats. Wholegrains. Variety of color berries like blueberries, raspberries, red cherries, aronia, dragon fruit, Indian gooseberries (Amalaki), and green tea. Herbs like thyme and rosemary. Cruciferous vegetables, … Beetroot juice (blood supply to the kidneys). (42) **A lot of color on the plate** (bioflavonoids[14] = antioxidants). **"Eat the rainbow."**
— **Flaxseed** (fiber and detoxification and Omega 3). (42)
— **Limit** (white, refined) **sugars** (also hidden in processed food). Get rid of sweet taste addiction. Dr. Joel Fuhrman: "sugar has taken and destroyed more lives than any other addiction." (Free) sugar is not food. It behaves like a chemical or a drug. (120)
— **Limit meat**, especially red meat and processed meat. (42) WHO has classified processed meat as a class 1 carcinogen, i.e., it is known to cause cancer. Reduce salt (2-3 grams daily, max. 5 grams or ⅞ of a teaspoon). Limit animal saturated fats (including hidden ones) and proteins. Favor olive oil and avocados. Get Omega 3 fats from food and possibly supplements.
— You may consider the DASH (Dietary Approaches to Stop Hypertension[15]) or PREDIMED (Prevención con Dieta Mediterránea) diet.[16] Another diet is MIND

---

13 Polyphenols are products of secondary metabolism of plants. There is flavonoid type (antokans, flavonoids, iso-flavonoids) and non- flavonoid (fenol acids, stilbenes, lignans, …). Polyphenols generally have positive effects on metabolism (anti-cancer, anti-inflammation, antioxidant). Gut bacteria convert polyphenols to a more easily absorbed form.

14 These substances include quercetin, hesperidin, eriodictyol, rutin, and naringenin.

15 It features vegetables, fruits, legumes, nuts, and whole grains, and limits foods that are high in saturated fat, such as fatty meats, full-fat dairy products, and tropical oils (coconut, palm kernel, and palm oils) as well as sugar-sweetened beverages, sweets, and high sodium foods. Many experts say, however, although the DASH diet is popular for hypertension control, it's not necessarily the best. (125)

16 DASH diet, Mediterranean Diet, and the Ornish Diet - all feature a plant-rich approach. There's a good deal of evidence that a whole-foods, plant- based diet can significantly reduce the risk of hypertension. (125)

(Mediterranean-DASH Intervention for Neurodegenerative Delay).[17]

— **Diverse diet, no extremes.**
— You may consider buying organic for foods in the Dirty Dozen group, so you can avoid pesticide-laden vegetables and fruits. (You do not have to buy organic in the Clean Fifteen group.) (42) (44)

If a food is on the Dirty Dozen list, always choose organic. If it's on the Clean Fifteen list, organic is still possible, but if it's not available, you may choose non-organic. If your produce is not organic, make sure to wash it very well and peel it if possible.

Dirty Dozen:	Clean Fifteen:
— Strawberries	— Avocados
— Spinach	— Sweet corn
— Kale. Collard and mustard greens	— Pineapple
	— Onions
— Nectarines	— Papaya
— Apples	— Sweet peas (frozen)
— Grapes	— Asparagus
— Bell and hot peppers	— Honeydew melon
— Cherries	— Kiwi
— Peaches	— Cabbage
— Pears	— Mushrooms
— Celery	— Cantaloupe
— Tomatoes	— Mangoes
	— Watermelon
	— Sweet Potatoes

Source: Environmental Working Group's 2022 Shopper's Guide to Pesticides in Produce; EWG updates the list annually.

You can read more on dieting principles (and see the biochemical explanations) using the references list at the end of this book, like (7) or (22) or (42).

---

17 It recommends vegetables (especially leafy greens), nuts, berries, legumes, whole grains, fish, poultry, olive oil, and, for those interested, wine. The surprising thing is how well it works. (100)

Many people are interested in aphrodisiac meals. The good news is that a good sex life is connected to overall health, so all the advice shown applies here as well.

What is the Latest Knowledge on Alzheimer's Prevention?

Physical activity is crucial for maintaining a healthy brain. Regular activity has been shown to reduce the risk of Alzheimer's disease by as much as 30%. (157). Engaging in physical activities increases blood flow to the brain and encourages the growth of new neurons and connections, which can help combat the effects of aging and cognitive decline.

According to "Alzheimer's - The Science of Prevention," the top seven brain health foods are:
— Wild-caught salmon
— Blueberries
— Leafy green vegetables
— Avocado
— Fermented foods (such as kimchi, kefir, and sauerkraut)
— Prebiotic foods (chicory root, Jerusalem artichokes, garlic, onions)
— Nuts (117)

Sanjay Gupta believes people should take their brain health into their own hands. Starting today. What is good for the heart is also good for the brain. Alzheimer's disease begins in the brain decades before the first symptoms appear. People at risk have plenty of time to do something about it. One in three appearances could be prevented by doing everything right. Comprehensive lifestyle changes are the concept for 21st century Alzheimer's disease prevention or slowdown. Your diet in your youth can be the foundation for protecting your brain in your Third Act. (100)

You do not need to visit a specialized clinic for basic information about preventing brain disease or to introduce even simple lifestyle changes that would delay the onset of disease, or at least alleviate its symptoms. (100)

Is all this too complicated?

You may be thinking it is all too complex. The good news is there is not one diet for fighting cancer, another diet for fighting Alzheimer's, another for heart disease, inflammation, infections, pathogens... **The same basic dietary pattern is good for all of the conditions. (42) And every little step helps.** You do not have to transition all of a sudden; even 10-20% changes will bring effects soon. You will feel better. Start with upgrading one meal. Find recipes. Hold on and continue making small changes incrementally. **Substitute out the old habits for the new ones one at a time. Think long-term. Start small, grow large.** You will rewire your microbiome, brain, saliva, shopping list — one step at a time.

Nutritional science has made significant advances in the last decade. We have the information to give people the opportunity to live into later years (age 95 or more) without dementia, cancers, heart attacks, strokes, or autoimmune issues.

More good news is that as of new research by Sandrine Thuret, we as adults can grow new brain cells ("neurogenesis"), improving mood, increasing memory formation, and preventing the decline associated with aging. The measures are mostly the same as mentioned above. (89)

It takes some time, energy, and planning. And if you think you do not have time to eat healthy, then where are you going to find the time to be sick?

Why shouldn't I improve my financial position by saving on food?

It is a myth that healthy food has to be more expensive. There are very beneficial foods that are super healthy and super affordable (and not super advertised[18]). Think of quinoa, soybeans, legumes, dark leafy vegetables, cabbage, etc. See above. Also, cut out waste.

Sometimes people who are making a switch to healthier eating will remark that plant-based diets seem deprived of flavor. But that will change over time, and actually, it will change very quickly because your taste buds completely regenerate in just two weeks. (121)

Hippocrates: "Let food be thy medicine."

The connection between the brain and the colon through a network of neurons and hormones is called the brain-gut axis. It works both ways. It means the microbiota can influence the brain. It's time to stop thinking of the organs of the body in isolation. The body is a complex interconnected system. All the more reason to keep the microbiota healthy. See the recommendations above.

Let me mention four more topics.

Probiotics

A probiotic is a living organism added to food or feed to benefit the health of the consumer by improving the balance of their intestinal microflora. Probiotics do benefit people. However, it turns out that in order to witness their true effect, it is better to take them as prevention rather than treatment. What does this imply? Consider taking probiotic or prebiotic supplements. You may consider trying for a week to see what works for you — you'll know by regular and easy bowel movements. If not, there is something wrong with your gut that needs more investigation.

I would like to add that I read scientific evidence on probiotics is not strong enough yet, so your first step should always be improving your lifestyle, eating nutrient-rich, fermented, and fiber-rich foods, adding exercise, and getting enough sleep.

---

18 Superfood has no medical significance. It suggests that it should be something very healthy, but it is a marketing term used by the food industry to sell. No food alone has such magical power to heal the brain or protect its health. The beneficial health effects are achieved by a combination of foods and nutrients. (100)

Food Intolerance and Lactose

You may have some food intolerance. (Your body doesn't digest a particular food or food group well.)[19] An estimated 15-20% of the population has one or more food intolerances. They can cause both gastrointestinal symptoms and a feeling of being tired all the time. The most common food intolerances include dairy (lactose) and gluten, but you can experience sensitivity to any type of food. You may want to work through an elimination diet (keeping a food diary), cutting back on foods one by one until you find the culprit(s). There are also tests available to check for food sensitivities. See below. (46) Food sensitivities appear to be one of the most obvious causes of autoimmune diseases, perhaps by causing inflammation.

If you experience frequent heartburn and possibly reflux, lactose intolerance may be the cause. (Reportedly 20% of people have it.) Dairy is scary. Eliminate cow's milk. Try lactose-free foods. There are plenty of them. Sour dairy products like yogurt and cottage cheese are better than whole milk, even for people without allergies. If you're not sure, it's always best to avoid milk, especially in the second half of life as the lactase enzyme (which breaks down milk sugar) decreases. It is advisable to limit all dairy products. (You can supplement protein with goat or sheep milk and plant proteins.) (21)

If you think you might have a gluten sensitivity, try gluten-free foods and see how you feel. There is already a very wide and tasty selection.

The top seven food intolerances are: gluten, dairy, eggs, soy, corn, peanuts, and sweeteners. (64)

Genomic Sequencing

If you want to do a lot for yourself, consider getting food intolerance testing (food IgG test), genetic or genomic sequencing of your gut microbiota (microbiome testing, stool test), and possibly a blood test to detect food intolerances

---

19 Food sensitivities and allergies are due to an immune response to a certain food when the immune system mistakes it for something harmful. Food intolerances don't involve the immune system. They are due to an inability to digest or metabolize a certain food.

that cannot be detected otherwise. Good interpretation of the results is important here.

Personally, I did food intolerance testing several years ago, followed by radical diet modifications, which has helped me with a lot of problems and improved my immunity and fitness. My digestive problems disappeared, I haven't had the flu for several years, and my happiness improved, too. This investment also had a side effect — it became a psychological commitment that enabled me to make sudden dietary changes that I wouldn't have decided to do otherwise.

Summary
Restoring microbial balance is a new area of medicine full of uncertainties. Whatever the potential of probiotics, prebiotics, and microbial ecosystem therapies for medicine, the old adage that **an ounce of prevention is worth a pound of cure** holds true. Humanity is going through decades in which we are gradually losing the microbial diversity that makes us human. What the human gut microbiota is actually "supposed" to look like scientists are only now learning in the few remaining societies that live in some completely untouched parts of the world without antibiotics and fast food. Now it's our turn to take a different path. I have provided you the recommendations, and I can say they helped me.

If you want to make an **estimate of your life expectancy** according to a few health and lifestyle questions, you can try it at https://www.livingto100.com/.

Microbiota in Old Age

From about the age of 60, the flora begins to change. The number of Bifidobacteria decreases, and the pH changes to alkaline. A particular form of Clostridia, NDH, causes a breeding ground for cancer-causing germs. In addition, the diets of older people tend to contain mostly protein and fat and physical activity decreases. This is leading to an increased incidence of bowel cancer, which is high in some countries. (There are intensive efforts to reverse this trend through early diagnosis and hemoccult tests.) (21)

The microbiota also degenerates with age (immuno-senescence). One of the manifestations is a chronic pro-inflammatory state (inflammageing). It is associated with diseases such as arthritis and Alzheimer's disease. (22) Many microbes themselves trigger inflammation. Reduced fiber intake (often, for instance, in nursing homes) and less exercise contribute to this. What is there to do about it? Eat more fiber. Limit saturated animal fats. Exercise. Movement is extremely important in old age (even if your motivation wanes). Exercise slows aging and reduces the risk of major diseases, including obesity, heart disease, diabetes, and even depression. It also reduces immunosenescence and chronic pro-inflammatory conditions. **The combination of a healthy diet and exercise is ideal.**

It is possible that a well-maintained microbiota can influence the aging immune system and keep the body in a younger state for longer. **It is** also **possible that the mystery of longevity lies in the optimal symbiosis of human cells and microbes.** (Research is still ongoing.) (22)

Taher Batterywala: "Many think they need the energy to exercise. But the truth is they need to exercise to have energy."

A few years ago, I started a (bi)daily habit to walk through a forest nearby, at least 4 km, with my friend. It was especially useful during the pandemic lockdown, with direct visible impact on my mood. I expanded this habit to organizing weekly cycling trips and cross-country skiing in winter as soon as the lockdown ended. Sometimes I help my friends organize orienteering runs. I have discovered without these activities I was often exhausted. Now I feel much better and get exhausted only after 50 km on bike or 20 km cross-country skiing.

When you start moving, it prepares you to move more, and your energy goes up. Moving is the fountain of youth. The more you move, the more energy you have. You get more energy, and it makes you feel useful again because now you don't use the excuse of being tired. You can do it, too.

Sex in Old Age

How will sexual life be after 60? Of course, not everything is as it used to be. This can be considered an advantage, however. One can think, in the knowledge of one's own erotic history, "If I can't anymore, I don't have to anymore." One can cynically watch, with a certain amusement, the younger generation that still has to in order to have something to remember later.

Planting Your Health Tree

This is the third part of the health equation.

Most of these steps should be no surprise. We've known them for a long time. But we have forgotten or turned our backs on them, succumbing to comfort, convenience, instant gratification, the pace and stress of modern living, and just laziness.

Practical recommendations:
— **Get enough good quality sleep.**
   Sleep is anything but a waste of time. It is a state in which the body heals tissues, strengthens memory, and even grows. Sleeping enough supports neuroplasticity and increases memory. Sleeping brings brain detoxification and regeneration at the cellular level. Humans are the only mammals that voluntarily deprive themselves of enough sleep. Thirty-eight percent of adults feel chronically sleep deprived; 21.7% suffer from sleep disorders. (92)
   Buy a quality mattress and use the correct sleeping position. Everyone needs (ideally) 7-8 hours of quality sleep daily — deep sleep and REM phase with minimal interruptions, no apnea, and no snoring. Have your mouth shut when you sleep. Consider how blue light at bedtime

might bother you. Listen to your body. Limit TV viewing.

František Šťastný at his 101st birthday party: "I eat little. I sleep a lot. I don't speak to old men."

Gene Perret: "I enjoy waking up and not having to go to work. So I do it three or four times a day."

According to sleepassociation.org, lack of sleep increases blood pressure, fat storage, bad decision making, depressive episodes, and the onset of ADHD. (92) Lack of sleep disrupts sugar levels. It can determine whether an individual will develop Alzheimer's disease. It puts you at greater risk for cardiovascular disease, contributes to depression, anxiety, and suicide. Lack of sleep promotes excessive appetite, leading to obesity. Overall, the less you sleep, the shorter your life. (28)

After a longer sleep, you eat less and healthier, you're in a better mood, you're happier, you communicate better with people, and you're more effective at work. Over time, you are less sick, have lower blood pressure, less need for medication, and have a lower weight. And you have better and happier relationships. So sleep is an important factor in prevention.

Many people suffer from obstructive sleep apnea (OSA). Approximately 20% of American adults suffer from it. In this disorder, soft tissues in the back of the throat cause the airway to narrow or close. The culprit may be being overweight, having large tonsils, or even just a certain shape of the throat. A person suffering from sleep apnea stops breathing for ten seconds to a minute or longer, which reduces the amount of oxygen in the blood and puts a strain on the heart. There are micro-awakenings, which can be hundreds a night, and this interrupted sleep does not allow the person to go through all the sleep cycles. It increases the risk of heart disease, diabetes, stroke, and cancer. Ninety percent of affected people are not diagnosed with this sleep disorder, however. It is more common in people over the age of fifty. It can be treated but must first be diagnosed (in a sleep laboratory). (100)

- Have control over the **glucose level in your blood** (70-130). High levels later lead to brain inflammation, cognitive decline, and possibly dementia and Alzheimer's. (42)
- Drink enough pure, clean water (not sweetened or from plastic bottles). Get **enough hydration**. A rule of thumb is that if you are already thirsty, you have waited too long. (Our brain is not very good at differentiating hunger from thirst, so if there is food available, we prefer eating. Consequently, we walk around the world overfed and chronically dehydrated. (100) Consider water filtration/purification from toxins.
- **Go outside**. "Forest bathing." (42)
- Consider **all of forms of rest**: mental, mindfulness, sensory rest (no headphones, dark), emotional (rest from strong emotions), spiritual (making myself sure that what I'm doing makes sense to me). Saundra Dalton Smith talks about up to seven forms of rest in her quite famous TED Talk.
- Don't skip the daily rest periods — 20 minutes after every 60-90 minutes of work. Don't miss weekends or holidays.
- Support metabolism. Lose weight. Eat a proper diet. Rehabilitate. Drink tea.
- Consider occasionally consulting with a physiotherapist and a nutritionist.
- Take a moment to work through the following questions and suggestions (complete with your partner if you have one): (34)
  - Are you able to maintain your health without any financial stress?
  - Is your level of physical activity higher or lower now than it used to be?
  - If you're about to retire, do you anticipate an active lifestyle?
  - What are some physical recreational activities that you both enjoy?

- What is a recreational activity you've never tried but deep down always wanted to try?

What do we know about the importance of exercise and movement?

Sitting for long periods of time causes excess weight, chronic problems (metabolic syndrome, heart problems, diabetes, etc.), mental issues, neck and spinal pain, digestive complications, and other health and economic complications. (122)

I do not have time to exercise. What can I do?

Those who want to maintain a strong mind understand the mind/body connection. When we treat ourselves well physically, our brains and minds benefit. We are far more vulnerable to unhealthy thinking patterns when we haven't been in motion. Whenever you spend a lot of time staying still, you will find yourself feeling worse and worrying more. Life is motion.

Human nature dictates that we fill all the time available to us with working on a task. And if we need an extra hour, the first thing we tend to sacrifice is exercise. Don't.

Exercise supports better sleep, more energy, weight loss, reduced inflammation, reduced pain, and a longer and healthier life. We've all heard that exercise is critical to being healthy, but how often do you actually exercise? (59)

Eighty percent of American adults do not meet the government's national physical activity recommendations for aerobic activity and muscle strengthening. Around 45% of adults are not sufficiently active to achieve health benefits. (88)

More than 70% of Americans 50 and older say they have joint pain according to a new survey, and 80% of them believe arthritis and joint pain are a normal part of aging. This perception, while it holds a grain of truth, obscures a rapidly growing reality: More and more people here and around the globe ignore the No. 1 recommended preventive measure for arthritis — physical activity. (81)

Global cases of osteoarthritis, sometimes called "wear

and tear arthritis" and the most common form of the condition, have more than doubled in the past three decades. While 64% of older Americans with arthritis or joint pain say they use exercise to mitigate their pain, and 80% of them rated their exercise as helpful, more than a third of sufferers don't exercise. Many turn to other less helpful approaches that come with potentially serious side effects.

The American College of Rheumatology recommends exercise and other physical activity above all other remedies for osteoarthritis. Weight loss is also atop the list. A combination of physical activity and improved diet can help people lose weight. The message from top doctors, scientists, and medical organizations: Look to physical activity, healthy eating, and other lifestyle remedies before turning to drugs. And whether you're young or old, in pain now or not, experts all agree there's no better time to get moving than today. Not just to lower your risk of joint pain but to improve your mood and physical health overall. (81)

As a young boy, I always hated exercise, and despite advice from doctors and pressure from my parents, I resisted and preferred sitting at home. My later profession increased the amount of time sitting at the table in front of PC screen to 10-12 hours a day. I developed poor spinal posture and back pain, followed by joint pain. I noticed a tendency to gain weight. In later years, I started skiing (downhill and cross-country), cycling, swimming, and mountaineering on a recreational level. Together with healthy dieting, I have noticed improvement in digestion, physical condition, back pain (nearly none), and mood, with positive impact on my relationships. Small, consistent, daily habits lead to long-term progress and results, which I am trying to maintain in my retirement, too.

Graffiti writer: "If you do not take care of your body, where do you intend to live?"

Most people take better care of their houses or cars than they do their own bodies. (31) The most exercise they get is lifting a glass of beer. It is very easy to find an excuse for not exercising. Anyone can start exercising at any age. In a survey, 45% of retired Canadians said they increased their physical activity after leaving work. You can, too. **The times that you do not want to exercise are the times you need it most.** Motivation and discipline are the key. You must consciously force yourself to overcome any excuses. The first 10 minutes of any physical activity are always the hardest. Simply make the decision and do it. You will be happy twice — first for making the decision and then for the benefits of exercising.

Find something you love that helps you move every single day. There's something for everyone, and it will add years to your life and life to your years! (59)

I heard a coach often saying: "It doesn't matter how you feel. It's what you do." He refers to that in everything he wants to reach, including exercise. Nobody likes to wake up in the morning saying, "I can't wait to work out" — except him. It's not about how you feel. He just does it, and then when he is done, he feels good because he has done it.

Discipline = making yourself do what needs to be done, when it needs to be done, whether you feel like it or not.

Marisa Murgatroyd: **"Consistency beats motivation."**

The good news: **All it takes is a few lifestyle changes.** If you dedicate 30 minutes a day to exercise (including walking), you'll be among the healthiest people. If you do 60 minutes 5 times a week, you will be among the top 2% healthiest people. (31) Find something you enjoy. Possibly exercise with someone. Twenty to sixty minutes of continuous aerobic exercise three or more times a week will do — running, brisk walking, swimming, or dancing. Reconnect with nature. You must do something physical every day.

The U.S. Department of Health and Human Services Physical Activity Guidelines for Americans recommends that for substantial health benefits and to reduce the risk of chronic diseases, including cancer, adults should engage in:

— 150 to 300 minutes of moderate intensity aerobic activity, 75 to 100 minutes of vigorous aerobic activity, or an equivalent combination of each intensity each week. This physical activity can be done in episodes of any length.

— Muscle strengthening (or strength training) activities at least 2 days a week.

— And balance training, in addition to aerobic and muscle-strengthening activity. (57) (59)

Remind yourself **daily** of your deeper reasons for committing to the process. What's your deeper reason? Is it to live longer, healthier, and with more purpose? To enjoy the remaining years of your life with more energy, happiness, and vitality? (59)

Put as much activity into your daily life as possible. Look for movement possibilities throughout the day. Some tips as a minimum:

— **Stand if you can, not sit**. Take small breaks during the day to stand, get away from your computer, stretch, and focus your eyes on distant objects.

— **Move if sitting.** The healthiest sitting position is the next one.

— **Use the stairs, not an elevator.** Try to walk at least 20 floors up a day.

— **Walk as much as possible.** Make at least 10,000 steps, which burns 300-500 kcal. Consider Nordic walking. The benefits of going for a walk exceed the physical ones. Walking starts the brain, and it then generates new thoughts. **Each step counts.** Be productive at the same time — produce something (things, relationships). Have fun.

— **Park far away.**

— Get up and get out! At least rediscover the joys of walking.

— Take smoke breaks at work, even if you do not smoke, just to go outside and move. (And did I mention that very important decisions are often made at smoke breaks?)

— **Incorporate some daily exercise into your routine.** If a gym is not accessible or you hate it, bike ride through your neighborhood or local park every morning or include a weekly round of golf or tennis lessons. Try to connect walking to exploring your environment. Outside exercise with fresh air prevents COVID spread. (31), (34).

Old saying: "If you do not make time for wellness, you will be forced to make time for illness."

☐ **Action step:**
Try to catch yourself: Put your workout, running clothes, or cycling trousers next to your bed. As soon as you get up, slip into it — before you know it, you're halfway through your workout. I can assure you; you'll feel great and more creative after your workout. Try to remember why you did it. What is the goal? What is the ideal result?

Robin Sharma: "Win the morning, win the day."

— Practice **balance stability**. I highly recommend studying a top expert, Pavel Kolář. (8)
— Take care of your **teeth**.
— Watch out for cataracts.
— In addition to a healthy balanced diet and exercise, **satisfying social relationships** also improve health. This combination has a range of impacts, from maintaining muscle mass to feeling a sense of purpose in life. There is a link between a **wide social network** and good health. (Science has only recently begun to explore this.) Microbes, even gut microbes, are everywhere. We pass them on when we interact with others. It has already been shown in mice that placing lean mice with obese mice allowed the "lean" microbes to infiltrate the obese mice and protect them from getting fat. How this is among humans is not yet proven, but beware the importance of social bonds during aging.

Strange as it seems, the now proven idea of the gut microbiota's influence on obesity looked strange years ago.

— For seniors, lower calorie requirements are sufficient, and the emphasis on **fruits, vegetables, fiber, and legumes** is even stronger. Specialized probiotics are in development. Until then, try to test what works for you.
— Prevention of **neurodegenerative diseases: controlled blood pressure, not smoking, not drinking too much alcohol, proper nutrition, exercise**, social contacts. Psychological prevention: **Keep the brain as busy as possible.**
— **Sharpen your senses**. (8)
— Take care of yourself calmly. Deep **relaxation**.
— **Spa** as health prevention (programmed rest, sleep, natural remedies, regeneration, especially after stress; resetting what you don't need in your head).
— Infrared sauna (learn more about the benefits here: (123)
— **Consider fasting**. Simple fast involves 12 hours of fasting including your overnight sleep. You can then slowly increase your fasting time. For instance, intermittent fasting 16 hours every day. (8 hours a day is the window for eating.) You can hear or read more about it in a few references at the end of this book: (21) (42) (93). Intermittent fasting increases autophagy, cellular rejuvenation, immune system function, and genetic repair. It reduces inflammation and the risk of disease. Like always, there is no one approach fits all, however. Everyone needs a different eating model. It also depends on the nature and life rhythm of the individual.

Find out what dietary model suits you and follow it accordingly. Long-term intermittent fasting does not lead to weight loss but rather to weight gain and an increased risk of obesity due to the danger of overeating. New diets will appear all the time, as there is a demand for them. No one wants to hear again that eating regularly and exercise really helps. If you are healthy, you may want to try intermittent fasting; however, do not strictly adhere to the hours when you "must" fast. If you are unbearably hungry, eat. Try to extend the fasting time, but do not overdo it. There is no need to eat five times a day. Eating three basic meals a day, with a five-hour break between meals, is optimal. (If you exercise for more than half an hour, you can include one more meal to compensate for the loss of nutrients.) (134)

Or at least shorten your feeding window from greater than 10-11 hours a day. (152).

- **Breathe properly**: Breathing properly, which is important, ensures all the muscles that attach to the trunk and pelvis, including the back, are extended in a controlled way. (8, page 81).
- Stay active. Move around. **Don't admit old age**.
- If you're doing any **sport** and are healthy, it's bound to hurt. We all know that studying or working hurts, too: Staying up late with books or going to work day after day is something we've learned to do. Most people today, however, trudge through life, and as soon as something hurts, they stop and have no motivation. When we stay in a space where we are just enjoying ourselves and not hurting, we lose a lot in life. With out strong inner motives, a person is weak. In today's age of excess, the motivation to overcome oneself is greatly diminished. What can we do about it? It takes going out of the comfort zone. It also leads to self-knowledge. (8)
- It takes a lifetime of sport and **adapting the load to your abilities**. It takes discipline. You can start any time. It's a little harder in retirement, but it's possible. **Move appropriately** to your capabilities. Do not laze or overexert. (4) Try swimming, cross-country skiing, cycling, Nordic walking, fast walking, or jogging.
- Suitable for the spine: **running, skating, swimming, dancing, weight training, stretching, or horse riding. Regular massages**.
- **Vitamins and supplements**: sun = vitamin D3 (also

in a supplement, 3,000-5,000 IUs[20] , as most people do not spend enough time in sunlight), B (esp. B12 supplement), K2 (at least 90 mcg), C, magnesium[21] , and calcium. Pairing vitamin D3 with K2 helps improve calcium absorption and control inflammation. Curcumin/turmeric (better for a short time in combination with black pepper). Collagen supplement. Green tea. You may consider resveratrol. But remember, the most important thing is the quality of your diet, which must do most of the work. You cannot supplement yourself to better health; supplements just fill in some little gaps. (14) (51) (59) (94)

— Be sure you get rid of toxins in your environment, e.g., mold, formaldehyde, dental amalgam (mercury) tooth fillings.

— **Mentally, do not slack off.** Do not get too stressed. Do not burn out. (4)

— Try **meditation**, yoga, Pilates, or Tai Chi.

— The complex, challenging (mostly brain and body) activities are good for neuroplasticity. Examples: dancing, playing musical instruments, learning foreign languages, and cooking new recipes. (92)

— You may want to try the Feldenkrais Method (https://en.wikipedia.org/wiki/Feldenkrais_Method).

---

20 When supplementing, opt for vitamin D3, also known as cholecalciferol, rather than vitamin D2, or ergocalciferol. Vitamin D3 is believed to be much more absorbable by the body. In addition, look for vitamin K2, magnesium, boron, and zinc to help with absorption. Because vitamin D is a fat-soluble vitamin, it is absorbed better when we take it with a fatty or large meal.

21 The RDA for magnesium range for males over 14 years of age: 400-420 mg/day. Close to 80% of our population is not getting this level. Top magnesium-rich foods are: swiss chard, spinach, grass-fed dairy, avocados, pumpkin seeds, sea vegetables, pink salts, nuts, dark chocolate, wild-caught fish, sprouts, and coffee. Supplemental magnesium is recommended for the majority of people. (129)

I'm sure I'm not telling you anything you don't already know. You know what to do. Do you really practice it? If you do, congratulations. If you don't, then you must choose what you are willing to apply. Please realize that neglect adds up over the years and backfires. I assume if you've read or listened this far, you want to do something for the cause.

Start small and slow. You may want to focus on one meal and think how you can improve it. You may also use the 80/20 rule, where 20% changes will bring you 80% benefits.

The Serenity Prayer: "Change what you can, accept what you must, but know the difference."

☐ Homework: Decide which steps you want to take.

_____

_____

_____

Then **include them in your list of goals**. And take your time. It's not going to happen overnight. Add progressively, not all at once, one thing first and keep momentum. (51)

Watering Your Health Tree

Let's use the **19-Action-Steps System to create your Health Plan**.

Are you ready to take the health challenge?

The action steps below are listed in no special order. Take one of these steps and focus on it. Incorporate it into your life. Do the action or make it a habit. Mark the checkbox then. Select another action and start it. Take them one at a time. Be kind to yourself, knowing that some of these changes will be more challenging than others.

☐ **Action step**: First, choose to be fit and healthy. Decide today that you **accept full responsibility for your health**. Don't complain about anyone or anything.

☐ **Action step**: Have a **full medical examination** (as soon as you can). Follow the doctor's advice.

☐ **Action step**: Decide that in a few months you will **reach the best shape you have ever had**. Get started. Don't make any excuses.

☐ **Action step**: Find 1 hour a day for yourself (movement). Start with **walking 30 minutes a day**. Take an extra bus station. Take the stairs, not the elevator. And so on.

☐ **Action step**: Think about **what you're not doing and should be doing in health**. You probably already know. What do you hide from yourself the most? Bring it to your consciousness. And then make commitments, write it into your goals, and go for it with determination... Be hard on yourself. This is about the most important person — you.

☐ **Action step**: Identify **a step that would increase the probability of living to 90 years** or more. Make this step.

☐ **Action step**: Consider hiring a **personal trainer** to push you. If you are starting out on your own, don't overdo it at first. Rather, be patient and persistent.

☐ **Action step**: Make sure that digestion is functional from top to bottom. Look at your thoughts about food. Are you eating under stress? Look at the oral microbiome and the state of your mouth. Look at every stage that is overlooked. **Change your diet** if you are eating unhealthily. Go for it immediately, **hold on for a month**, and you'll see that you'll get used to it. Hang in there. You can expect improvement or **substantial improvement after about half a year**.

☐ **Action step: Stop rewarding yourself with food** (for life's hardships, for stress, for disagreements, etc.). Solve the causes instead, maybe with the help of a coach.

☐ **Action step**: **Plan** your **meals** in advance. Don't let hunger surprise you. When you're not ready, deep-seated animal instincts start pushing you in the wrong direction toward anything that's fast, tasty, and gratifying. Try to carefully plan buying the meals at least twice a week. Keep the principles mentioned in this chapter.

☐ **Action step**: How will my sexual life be after 60? **Can you imagine your sexual life after 60 or admit that it will eventually come to an end?** What steps and/or routines do you need to take now? Add them to your list of goals.

☐ **Action step**: Consider **investing in yourself**: a comprehensive cancer prevention program. Alternatively, food intolerance testing, gut microbiome testing (DNA testing), and inflammatory tests, followed by comprehensive lifestyle changes, diet, and possibly treatment.

☐ **Action step**: Go back to your written goals. **Write down the activities you will start doing or stop doing** to achieve excellent health.

Are these goals [PEVS][22] ? Adjust your goals if necessary.

What will it mean to you that when you retire, your health will be as good as possible? What else will such a state allow you to do?

☐ **Action step**: What **expert or other help** do you need to do this?

---

22 Positive; Exciting and Emotional — you really want it; Visualized; and unrealistic - a little Scary. They will thus become motivating and push you out of your comfort zone.

☐ **Action step: What one first step, however small, would have the biggest positive impact** on meeting your health plan? Write it down immediately, include a reminder to your calendar / mirror / refrigerator, and do it.

☐ **Action step**: What will be the **next steps** or activities? What will you do to get them adopted? What is the best you have to give?

☐ **Action step**: Put **weekly reminders into your calendar** to accomplish this task. What gets scheduled gets done. Always ask: which other activity would add the most value to this goal?

☐ **Action step**: Take another look at your written goals. Make them **daily habits and routines**. And have in mind all habits (good or bad, big or the most trivial). A habit loop works: Stimulus -> Desire -> Reaction -> Reward. (23) Every habit can be learned. (A side effect is that a good new habit will displace an old bad one). Start each day with the most important habit. (Even if anything else fails that day, you'll be satisfied.) It takes discipline. Without it, nothing will get done. (Discipline = making yourself do what needs to be done, when it needs to be done, whether you feel like it or not.) Anyone who has clarity of goals can do it.

☐ **Action step**: Describe the **three biggest fears or barriers** you are currently experiencing in this area. What would you do if success was guaranteed?

People who choose to do something for their health often do so for specific reasons, such as "I want to live longer without illness" or "I want to have the best retirement possible." Keep in mind why you are doing all this. Not only will a healthy lifestyle be easier to maintain, but you'll return to it if you ever get off track. It's true: **Progress is better than perfection**. (100)

You may wonder, *How can I manage all this?* I know change can be hard to start. I did it once, too. But once you get started, it becomes easier. Take one thing, possibly what you feel you need most or what is easiest to start with, and do it until you feel like you're ready to take on another step. Build your habits. Do not only rely on your willpower. (Consistency beats motivation). And then do not stay only with the steps you already do, as you would not get the new results you want. Taking on new action steps takes strength. And you will see changing the little things can lead to big results and a huge difference in your life.

If you have a significant other, do it with your significant other. Support each other. It is more fun to do it together. Find supportive systems and networks with same values (communities, online, etc.).

Do not use unhealthy eating for comfort or reassurance of self-love. Nurture yourself using other means.

Only reading means nothing. But if you act, these things will work. How do I know? I have incorporated most of these things into my own life, and I have seen the positive changes. Now it's time for you to experience it.

Remember, this is not a quick fix. It's not about trying some small changes, and then thinking you can get back to eating and living unhealthy again. Anti-aging is a skill anyone can work on each day.

Be the CEO of your health.

If you take it honestly, you probably won't just create a series of steps and routines to meet your goals but a **new lifestyle** — one that will add years to your life and quality to those years.

Enjoy Your Third Act: Signs of Luxury in Retirement

The ideal is to **get into a state of wealth and luxury** with the following symptoms:

— The degree to which **I can dispose of my free time**.
— The ability and opportunity to **pay attention to what I choose**.
— The ability **not** to **go with the mainstream**.
— **Ownership of a private space** that is not invaded by anyone I don't want there.

In short: **I can do what I want, when I want, with whom I want, where I want, for how long I want.**

Visit **www.livingyourbestthirdact.com**. You will find free templates, exercises, checklists, outlines, worksheets, and physical action plans.

THIRD ACT
RESOURCES

Chapter 7: Managing Stress

This chapter will provide an overview of methods for managing stress, in case you need it.

When I wrote this book, I wasn't sure whether stress would be part of the health chapter because they are so interconnected. When I first read it, it made sense, but I see now it needs its own separate attention because I don't like overwhelming people, as overwhelm equals inaction, and I want people to be in (proper) action and not be overwhelmed, which would add even more stress.

After learning how important it is to take care of the physical part of you in the previous chapter, the stress part of your life will be less stressful, as the physical and the emotional are connected. I will show you now other things you can do to help manage stress.

Stress will be there in your life, no matter what and no matter what age. The more proactive you are, the less impact it generally has.

On the other hand, we need a certain amount of good stress (is time limited and has a victory at the end) at any age, otherwise our resilience and performance will decline. This is most noticeable with the elderly. If they are efficient and take care of themselves or are mentally active, they function. If they slacken the demands on themselves, they deteriorate mentally and physically. It may go quickly then.

Excessive stress, on the other hand, can have a very negative impact on all areas of life. Prolonged psychological stress not only affects our psyche but also our posture. It also affects the immune system, central nervous system, and the hormonal system. The immune and cardiovascular systems deteriorate and autoimmune diseases, back pain, and even cancer can result. Stress can increase our opportunities to make poor choices. We are more likely not to exercise, possibly smoke more, and eat things we otherwise would not eat. (42)

I find that stress sometimes gets talked about in an incorrect way. People think decreasing stress means to just relax. But it is about knowing how to understand your emotions and use proper emotions at the proper time.

Your life may look like constantly battling for survival. Perhaps money is coming in, and you are successful. Then your Third Act comes, and suddenly you have limited resources to live on, your health isn't really as good as it could be, your relationships fall apart, and you don't know what to do with your life. It is a hell of a lot of stress, and stress will change your whole outlook on your Third Act, more than anything else in your life. All the things combined are important. Stress is the trigger point, and if you don't listen to what stress is telling you and understand how it is or is not beneficial, the whole house of cards can come falling down.

Let's discuss major schools of approach to stress management.

Stress management according to Positive Intelligence

(Shirzad Chamine):

All stress is caused by your saboteurs. However, if you **engage your sage**, you will accomplish your tasks but not get so stressed. You will know that **every result can be turned into a gift or opportunity**, including serious mistakes and setbacks. You won't be so dependent on the outcome, and this will reduce stress. **By using the positive thinking parts of your brain, you won't feel stress even in life's biggest storms**. (20)

□ **Action step**: If you are interested in a short introduction on inner saboteurs, see https://www.youtube.com/watch?v=-zdJ1ubvoXs (20-minute TEDx Talk video)

You can discover your top saboteur, or test your saboteurs, here: https://assessment.positiveintelligence.com/saboteur/overview or https://assessment.positiveintelligence.com/pq/overview). Then learn to strengthen your sage. It's best done with a good coach.

The Basic Coaching Approach to Stress Management

Coaching books are saying that chronic stress lasting weeks or months, constant tension, poor digestion, weight gain, and so on can be addressed with a coach. (At the latest at the beginning of the depression; a coach cannot help with the permanent depression).

It is necessary to **find answers to three questions**:

1.   **What can I not control?**
2.   **What would I like to have under control?**
3.   **What could I do but don't do?**

You may be going in circles between 1) and 2); that's the stressor. You need to figure out what you're going to do to get out of this cycle. Separate what you can control from what you cannot, then focus exclusively on the former. It's always long-term. You're always in control of yourself. **It's always up to you how you live the rest of your life**.

You may want to download a tool from **www.livingyourbestthirdact.com**: Premeditatio malorum.pdf

"Not Having Enough Time": A Source of Stress

Another belief that causes tremendous stress for people, continuously activating fight or flight, is time — the **destructive belief is "not having enough of it."** I watch most managers torture themselves daily with this belief. They are **always rushing**, always stressing, always wanting to be somewhere else, be perfectly on time, be there, not here, not accepting life as it is, feeling like they are missing out, feeling like once they get there, they will be happy, but here, they are not happy. (57)

Once you can **let go of your attachment to time and learn to appreciate every single moment**, whether you're where you want to be right now or not, then life becomes so much more joyful, and a great bonus is that your immune system is kicked on, and your body heals.

Other Approaches to Managing Excessive Stress

(To the see the full color picture go to www.livingyourbestthirdact.com)

Register stress (**acknowledge it**) and compensate for it (i.e., **action is required!**) with the right amount of **rest** (it's about balance), **proper breathing, sports, nature, cold showers, change of diet**, and endure it repeatedly.

Decrease your stress reaction one step at a time. You can manage it step-by-step, but if you never take a step, you'll never get it done. Select a stress reaction step from the picture above and do it.

Make a **gratitude journal** (see separate action step later). Take a moment to feel gratitude for things in your life you may take for granted, as often as you can. This is different than waiting for big successes and accomplishments to feel happy. (20) Have a "**master list**" (not to worry about forgetting something).

For sorting out work tasks, you may use the **MoSCoW** agile project management method. (Classify your tasks as: **Must have, Should have, Could have, Won't have**.) (146)

Learn how to **say no**.

Make a list in two minutes in the morning:
- **I'll concentrate on...**
- **I'm grateful for...**
- **I'll pass on...** (12)

Don't multitask. **Focus on one task.** (You need to know what is essential and important; alternatively, you can start with the most annoying one.) Get yourself into a flow, rest, and then go to the next task.

Learn how to avoid stressful and annoying people. Balance your possible obligations and the minimum necessary level of stress.

Consider learning **mindfulness**. There are several mindfulness modes. See if you are comfortable with working alone in silence, meditating on your body or your breath, with music, or with the spoken word. You can find plenty about this online. Try what works for you.[23]

Stress is largely a choice. While we do not have total control over the thoughts that pop into our heads (about 65,000 of them per day), we do have control over how we respond to them.

Stress management, all the other pillars, and Third Act planning are actually projects. And this project is yours. You are a project that you work on daily to become a better you. Whether it is reading, exercise, planning your diet, or handling your stress, it's all interconnected.

---

23 You may want to consider analytical meditation (suitable even for the most skeptical people). Think of a problem you want to have solved. Separate it from everything else by placing it into a transparent mental "bubble." It will then detach from any links, e.g., emotional ones. It will become isolated and will start to clarify. You will see practical solutions. (100)

Chapter 8: Your Social Plan - Relationships

"Your wealth is where your friends are." Titus Maccius Plautus

Do you realize the importance of relationships (family, friends, and wider communities) to your well-being, before and in retirement?

Your mission for this chapter — should you choose to accept it — is to prepare and start implementing a Retirement Social Plan, so you will enjoy decades of happy life and good relationships, before and during your Third Act. Imagine doing what you have planned for when you want, **with whom you want**, wherever you want, for as long as you want, when retired.

In this chapter, we discuss the Social Plan for your Third Act, plus the importance of relationships.

After reading this chapter, you will understand:
—   The distinct steps of the "social plan equation"
—   How to build and improve family relationships
—   How to plan for relationships with friends
     and wider communities
—   How to cope with great anger
—   The art of living alone, should you wish to do so
—   Action steps to bring it all together

The Social Plan Equation

To make the relationships topic clearer, I structured it into these distinct parts I have identified as being important. They are the "social plan equation":

1)   Family
2)   Friends and other communities
3)   Other useful tools
       — How to cope with great anger
       — The three R's method
       — The art of living alone, should you wish to do so
       — Approach to make friends at all levels

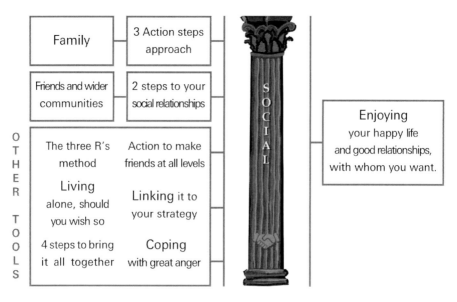

By improving your family relationships (using the 3-Action-Step approach), planning for friends and wider communities relationships (2- Action-Step approach), and using other tools and techniques, you will be prepared to enjoy decades of happy life and good relationships with whomever you want before and in your Third Act.

You will also get two bonus chapters, in case you need them.

What you can look forward to in retirement: You will no longer have full responsibility for your children as they will likely be adults and take care of themselves. You can pretty much enjoy them and your grandchildren, without having that high responsibility for them anymore. You will have resolved responsibility for your parents. (If they are alive, they are being cared for as comfortably as you would like yourself to be cared for later.) You maintain a good relationship with them. You are much more accountable to yourself than in previous stages. What you make, you'll have.

Dean Ornish (https://www.ornish.com/): People who are lonely and depressed and isolated are 3-10 times more likely to get sick and die prematurely in comparison to those who have loving connections and community.

Social isolation and feelings of loneliness are on the rise in our society. It is a paradox of our times: Thanks to digital media, we are more connected than ever before, yet we are distanced and suffer from loneliness because we lack authentic connections. The absence of real connections between people has become an epidemic, and medicine is gradually recognizing this condition has very serious physical, mental, and emotional consequences, especially among the elderly. (100)

There was a Harvard study in 1938 to determine the likelihood of a 50-year-old living to old age. The main indicator was not cholesterol but the quality of interpersonal relationships. "The clearest message that we get from this 75-year study is this: Good relationships keep us happier and healthier. Period." (65) It's not about how much is in your 401(k), how many tech companies you worked for and how much power you wielded there, or how many conferences you spoke at, etc. The biggest predictor of your happiness and fulfilment overall in life is, basically, love.

The study demonstrates that having someone to rely on helps your nervous system relax, your brain stay healthier for longer, and reduces both emotional as well as physical pain. Those who feel lonely are more likely to see their physical health decline earlier and die younger. "It's not just the number of friends you have, and it's not whether or not you're in a committed relationship. It's the quality of your close relationships that matters." (65) There are two foundational elements to this: One is love. The other is finding a way of coping with life that does not push love away.

As I see it, you could have all the money you've ever wanted, a successful career, and be in good physical health, but without loving relationships, you won't be happy. The good life is built with good relationships.

Sidney M. Jourard, psychologist and author of Healthy Personality, found that as much as 85% of your happiness will come from your relationships.

People with fewer social contacts suffer from disrupted sleep patterns, immune system disorders, inflammation, and higher levels of stress hormones. Isolation increases the risk of heart disease by 29% and the risk of stroke by 32%. (100)

People who spend most of their time alone have a 30% higher risk of death in the next seven years. This effect is most pronounced in middle age. For the elderly, loneliness has been shown to be primarily responsible for cognitive decline. These data urge us to care for our relationships in the same way we care for our health through diet and exercise. A quality social life is clearly very important to the basic functions of life. (100)

Baratunde Thurston: "I hacked my life-expectancy clock to help motivate me. Now instead of showing me how I can improve my life-span, it shows me how much longer I can live than the people I hate."

Marcel Proust: "Let us be grateful to the people who make us happy; they are the charming gardeners who make our souls blossom."

Family

Having close family or friends is an essential ingredient for a healthy and successful retirement.

The physical and psychological condition of a living spouse is of great importance to humans. The influence of close relationships, especially marriage, on the health of an individual is being studied both from the point of view of physical health and from the point of view of psychology. In the first six months after the loss of a spouse, widows and widowers have a 44% higher risk of death. The cause of this increased risk undoubtedly lies in part to the loss of a companion. (100)

Retirees are enjoying stronger relationships with family and loved ones because family is a core part of identity in retirement. According to them, the most important contributor to their identity in retirement is not their past work or finances — 61% say it's their "relationships with loved ones." (86)

Social isolation is linked to an increased risk of heart disease, dementia, and death. One in four adults aged 65 and older were socially isolated before the pandemic in the U.S. in 2020, i.e., they had little to no meaningful social contact, and COVID-19 only increased that figure. (86)

You may be thinking: *I can hardly put up with my spouse for several hours now. How will it be in retirement?*

"I married you for better or worse, but not for lunch every day" is becoming a popular motto among retired couples and those heading into retirement. Retirement planning needs to extend to include specific things couples can do to strengthen their relationship and minimize arguments. Expectations and assumptions about everyday life in retirement aren't always mutual. One study revealed that 75% of people near retirement, but still working, believe that their quality of life in retirement will improve, but only 40% of retirees found that it really did. That's grounds for disagreements.

Identifying different priorities is critically important, including how much time each wants to spend together and apart.

Couples need to keep in mind that just because one person

doesn't want to eat lunch with you every day, or spend every waking hour with grandkids, doesn't mean they don't love and care about you. Spending time apart can be healthy for a relationship because when people are given space to do the things that make them happy, they often bring that joy back into the marriage. (126)

One solution is to maintain a combined but separate social network. The spouse with a smaller social network may have more work to do before the Third Act to build and strengthen their social network. If this doesn't happen during the early phase of retirement, it might put a major burden on the relationship and on the spouse saddled with planning not only their own activities but their spouse's as well.

Mike Margolies: While discussing marriage and retirement with a group, an advisor raised a glass of water and asked, "How much does this glass of water weigh?" After fielding the standard answers, the advisor said, "The weight depends on how long you try to hold it. If you hold it for a minute, that's not a problem. If you hold it for an hour, your arm will ache. If you hold it for a day, you'll have to call an ambulance. In each case, it's the same weight, but the longer you hold it, the heavier it becomes. And that is the way it is with relationships in retirement. The longer you go without discussing your thoughts and plans and developing a set of shared expectations, the bigger and heavier the issues can become."

Sooner or later, unmet expectations or differences of opinion will turn into ongoing arguments or long-standing resentments, and you won't be able to hold them.

Do you live in peace with your children and grandchildren? Do they have something to talk about with you? Do they enjoy being with you?

Many people may not be clear on: *Will I still have responsibility for my children?*

Make clear for yourself what level of responsibility for your children (not just financial) you want to have. Of course, do not let them down in case of serious troubles, but too much care is harmful both for them and you.

What kind of lifestyle do I want for myself and my family in the Third Act? **Is my partner my best friend?** How can I improve my relationships with my partner, spouse, family, and children?

☐ Homework: Add the new goals and tasks to your list of goals while reading this chapter.

Decide which steps you want to make as an entry into your calendar.

For some steps, you may want to place a sticky note onto your refrigerator.

3-Action-Steps approach to improve your family relationships

☐ **Action step**: Every relationship changes over time. For it to be a change for the better, you must be prepared to change yourself. Without flexibility, it is impossible to have a long-term happy relationship. (19) Gather the courage to **ask your partner** (**and** then your **children**) these four questions. You will be surprised at the depth of the answers and the impact on your family life if you can follow through:

— Would you like me to do more of what I do?
— Would you like me to do less of what I do?
— Would you like me to start doing something?
— Would you like me to stop doing something altogether?
  Again, add the new relevant steps, goals, and tasks to your list of goals.

☐ **Action step**: Think about the main **qualities you want to instill in your children** and grandchildren and how you will achieve this. You have less time than you think. **Ask yourself:**

— If I were a **perfect role model** for them, how would I behave differently?
— What **mistakes** should I **forgive** my children? Do it now.
— What can I do to **spend more time** with my kids and grandchildren?
— How will I lead them to be more **self-disciplined**, and how will I reward them for it?

☐ **Action step**: How much do I want to **take care of my**

children and grandchildren in my Third Act? How do I want to take care of them in advance? Do I want to set up a suitable insurance policy (for instance, accident insurance) for them? Do I want to make a will? Do I want to place assets in a trust (and set the terms of withdrawal)?

Planning for Relationships with Friends and Wider Communities

Louis CK: "In times of need, you will know true friends. So hope you never get to know them."

Jim Rohn: "We are the average of the five people we spend the most time with."

A study at Brigham Young University concluded that a lack of good friends and connections can be as damaging to your health as smoking 15 cigarettes per day! (151)

You may be wondering: *I have my spouse, children, and a lot of friends. Why should I think of any extra relationships?*

Your closest friends and family group can be awfully little. In old age it is becoming clear that the psychological impact of losing all but the closest ties can be deep. A quality life is not an isolated affair experienced with only a few loved ones. **All forms of friendship are important**. Peripheral relationships connect us to the wider world. Otherwise, we fall into the monotony of closed networks.

Wider interactions reinforce our sense of community, of something larger. **People on the fringes of our lives** introduce us to new ideas, information, and opportunities. **Diversity is the spice of life.** And don't think if you're an introvert that this doesn't matter to you. (18)

This also includes being around younger people because of their vibrancy, excitement, energy, more positive outlook, and fresh views. By limiting yourself to your own generation, you miss a lot of opportunities in life to know more. You already know your Third Act is based on the idea of never-ending learning and curiosity.

You could become a mentor for younger people. This keeps you young. You can share with them what maybe they're not aware of because it wasn't part of their learning as a generation.

My father was a World War II veteran along with several friends. They fought against Nazis, commencing from the UK through France, alongside Canadian troops. One of his friends (who is still alive) is often invited to schools for discussions with young students. He enjoys sharing his experience, he feels needed and useful, and (as I have seen in person) students are really interested and ask very deep and clever questions. Such an activity really guides all involved to think deeply on basic life questions (and helps them to find answers).

Different types of relationships and social roles **can meet different needs**. Life without such interactions sometimes leads to a rise in conspiracy theories, with the conspiracy bubble as another source of isolation. If you only talk to people like yourself, your views become even further distanced from those of other groups of people. In extreme cases, cults may be formed. (18)

Investing in network building is of paramount importance. These connections provide help when you need it most and allow you to give back to others. (75)

To become a top networker, be curious about other people. Ask them about themselves. Let them talk about 70% of the time. Find out how you can help them accomplish their goals. The more you help them, the more likely it is they will reciprocate. Get outside your bubble. (75)

Andy Storch: "I want the other person to do most of the talking because then I get to learn more about them and how I can potentially help them."

You may think, *I have my opinions. Why should I meet people who disagree (and disturb my peace)?*
Get outside your bubble.
Ideally you should have support network(s), so you can discuss your problems with them. (18)

You may not find all the answers from people within your bubble. And most important, you will miss many important questions.

Even the physical consequences of isolation are documented. **Social isolation increases the risk of premature death by 30%.** If the social necessity of certain behaviors (hygiene habits, taking medication, taking care of oneself) is removed, some people lose the ability to perform even the basic tasks of life. Thus, loneliness also affects the body. In addition, no one may notice the signs of an incipient illness. (18)

You may think, *I do not have time/knowledge to make friends now. Can it be learned in retirement?*

Many retirees, more often men, can end up lonely, bored, and depressed if they did not develop real friendships. Moreover, they may have lost the skills to cultivate real friendships. Or they have neglected former good friends in favor of their careers. **They must spend more time and effort creating and maintaining friendships now.** (31)

People who exercised frequently had a 35 percent lower risk of dementia. Regular housework reduced it by up to 21 percent. And a social life by 15 percent. (162)

University of Kansas communication studies professor Jeffrey A. Hall quantified how much time we need to make a friend. To turn a stranger into a close friend, Hall says it takes 200 hours of intense getting-to-know-you time, ideally spread over six weeks. The fact that friendships take time to form is acknowledged by anyone who has ever experienced it. In the second act of life, as people build careers and start families, time becomes an increasingly scarce commodity, and building new friendships suddenly becomes an almost unattainable luxury. The consequences can be literally devastating in the Third Act. Strong relationships are one of the ingredients for a happy life. They determine our health and life satisfaction. It's a network that is essential for us. (90)

Sanjay Gupta believes seniors with a larger network of social contacts are better protected from the cognitive decline associated with Alzheimer's disease. Involvement in a large group is the best protection, especially if the group engages in a challenging activity. (100)

Therapist Michal Peter believes "time-tested closeness" is one of the best definitions of friendship. Anyone who wants to make friends at any age must meet a few conditions. Besides the two obvious ones (time and a feel for how to get around new people), there's a willingness to open up to the other person and talk about things we're usually afraid to share because of shame or fear that openness won't be reciprocated. "And that's tricky. And risky, and it takes courage, which is not easy to gather, at any age." But there's no other way. Without these elements, a solid bond is not formed. (90)

Retirees have to replace the sense of community that their company provided them with some other means of social contact. **The happiest seniors tend to be those who are experiencing community involvement** in such places as **clubs, churches, housing**, hobby, or sport **communities**. They live happier, healthier, and longer lives. The worst poverty is to be without any friends.

Modern Elder Academy: "Learn to become a guide or role model for others at all ages and stages of life who are also struggling. Remember, 'wisdom is not taught. It is shared.'"

The need to interact with others, **to feel wanted, and to have a sense of belonging** has more of an impact on retirement life because the impact is more immediate compared to health and financial concerns, which tend to set in over time.

Many people neglect to devote time to making close friends while they are working. For some people, retirement also detracts from the number of friends they end up having. It may be difficult to find like-minded people in your age group in your Third Act. **Develop a broad-based network while still employed.** Friendship is an active element that requires constant input for it to survive and thrive.

Ethel Barrymore: "The best time to make friends is before you need them."

A boy was sitting in a doctor's office waiting room and struck up a conversation with an old man sitting nearby. He asked him the usual questions: How are you? What brings you here today? The old man told the boy he was getting a regular check-up because he'd just turned 70. The boy asked the question that always comes to mind when we meet someone close to our grandparents' age: What are you grateful for? The old man thought for a moment and said,

"You know what I miss? Relationships." He explained: "I'm not talking about my wife or my kids. I have a great relationship with them. But all the other relationships are dead — friends, colleagues, work partners, neighbors, etc." It hit the boy like a ton of bricks. He realized he was taking his relationships for granted. He knew a lot of people, but he wasn't investing in them the way he should have been. The lesson is: Don't take your relationships for granted. Invest in them while you still can. (127)

We need a few close friends. **Keep company with people who are interested in the world outside themselves.** The nearer you are to your Third Act, the more important it is that the majority of your friends are not associated with your job. You need **at least two or three close, happy, and interesting friends with whom you can relate on a deeper level.** You share a number of interests unrelated to your career. You must be getting something of value from them, and they must be receiving something of equal value from you. Have your own friends. Do not rely on your spouse's friends only.

Have you become close enough to at least one new person in the last three years that you can talk, to the complete satisfaction of both of you, for half an hour about something unrelated to work?

The relevant question is: How do you attract, maintain, and manage vital relationships?

A True Friend:
— Continues to like you whether you end up rich or poor
— Likes you despite your achievements
— Will not abuse you in any way
— Will not take advantage of you in times of weakness
— Will not desert you when you are down
— Is someone with whom you can be sincere and vulnerable
— Is a confidant who won't tell your most personal secrets to someone else

- Will defend you in your absence when someone says something nasty about you
- Will get you to laugh when you become too serious about life
- Above all, a true friend reminds you of the person you would like to be.

Ralf Waldo Emerson: "The only way to have a friend is to be one."
Review the above list for yourself.

Some people may have another question: *How do you maintain a broad range of social connections (too many) in the Third Act?*

People may see it as too many commitments. How can I be a good friend to each person if I have so many of them? Research shows that more intelligent individuals experience lower life satisfaction with more frequent socialization with friends. People with higher levels of friendship satisfaction do not have more friends than those with lower levels of friendship satisfaction. (95)

Older participants reported smaller social networks, largely because of reporting fewer peripheral relationships. Yet older age was associated with better well-being. Although the reported number of close friends was unrelated to age, it was the main driver of well-being across the life-span. However, well-being was more strongly related to social satisfaction than to the reported number of close friends, suggesting it is the perception of relationship quality rather than quantity that is relevant to reporting better well-being. My suggestion then would be to consider what type of people you really want to attract into your life. And understand what you can learn from each of them. Then set up the amount of time and activities you spend with them accordingly. It is not your obligation to maintain a broad range of too many social connections.

Ask yourself: *Which three (or more) people matter most to me?*

What are **the implications of the pandemic?** It may create a desire for a strong-arm government (which will offer quick and completely wrong solutions). Sometimes collective trauma can completely dismantle communities, disrupting interpersonal relationships, traditions, and trust. As the experience of researchers shows, coping with collective trauma is helped by maintaining social ties, whether within the family, among friends, or otherwise. (25) As U.S. researchers studying the impact of the hurricanes that devastated Florida in 2004 and 2005 found, people who lived in **communities with close and strong social ties suffered far less** from depression and post-traumatic stress disorder. And therein lies one of the misfortunes of the current state. If we want to maintain our mental health, we need as close contact with people as possible. Try to preserve it as much as possible. If you can't see people physically, at least do it digitally using the phone, Zoom, webinars, interest groups, a virtual beer, etc. (25)

What friendships are built on:
1. **Time spent together.** 40-60 hours during the first 6 weeks for shallow friendship. 80-100 hours for a deep one.
2. **Attention.** Friendship can emerge anywhere any time if both sides are open to it. Look for friendships in places you would never expect it. Pay attention to your vicinity. Be open to chance encounters. It is never too late to meet someone who could play an important role in the rest of your life.
3. **Intention.** Be active. Seize the opportunity. It requires effort, energy, courage, a willingness to hide weak spots, and risking even embarrassing moments. Friendships need to be worked on.
4. **Rituals.** Regular meetings.
5. **Imagination.** Side role to main life roles (work, family, erotic relations). Diversity.
6. **Grace.** Flexibility to long pauses. Be able to overcome the absence of relations and forgive disappointments. (49)

2-Action-Steps approach to maintain or build your social relationships plan

☐ **Action step:** Don't underestimate social isolation. **What friendships do you want to maintain or build** in time for retirement? Do you want to make more friends? What can you do now? What can you do to make them feel comfortable with you? How can you use modern digital tools to find new friends? Put it in your list of goals.

Contrary to popular belief, **creating new friends in retirement is a skill that can be learned practically by everyone.** You must act and work on it. You cannot wait at home to be discovered. Take the initiative. **Adopt effective strategies** for making new friends. It takes practice. Participate in communal and social situations where you can share yourself with others. Go to where interesting people hang out. The more activities you get involved in outside your home, the more people you will meet, and the more probability you can meet new acquaintances and make friends. Practice your ability to give as well as receive. Show people how to be friendly. **Be interested in people rather than being interesting. Suspend judgement** of other people for at least a short time. People tend to surprise us if we give them a chance. Try to **have friends from all age groups.**

Add the new relevant steps, goals, and tasks to your list of goals.

☐ **Action step**: Try **six ways to make friends** (and good relationships with people in general):
1. **Accept people for who they are.** This doesn't mean you have to agree with them, but don't judge them, even unconsciously. **Non-judgmental observation.** Focus on the impression they make on you, instead of the impression you want to make on them.
2. **Appreciate them** for anything that deserves an appreciation. Sometimes all it takes is a **simple "thank you,"** a **nod**, or a **smile**. Sometimes a **thank-you email** is appropriate or a **gift**. Or you could use a very powerful tool: a handwritten **thank-you letter.**
3. **Agree with them.** Whenever you can. Even if you don't fully identify with it. **It's not about your ego. It's about the relationship.** No one is ever fully wrong;

everyone is at least 10% right. Never use the "Yes, but" approach. Use the **"Yes... and."** For example, "What I like about what you say is... And how about we additionally try..."

4.   **Show admiration.** Lincoln: "A compliment pleases everyone." Admiration for a look, a dress, a quality, an achievement, etc.

5.   **Pay attention. Use focused, empathetic listening.** It's a tremendous gift these days. Ask and then listen more than you talk.

6.   **Never criticize, never judge, never complain. Not even indirectly.** You'll only make relationships worse. If you want to give negative feedback, it's to be done differently. If you want to achieve a change in their behavior, this is a huge task that can be done by an excellent coach, and only if the person themselves wants to. You certainly won't achieve it by criticism. Your job is to **have them say you're "nice."**   (20)

What three words would you like others to use when describing you in your absence?

Other Useful Tools

Bonus: How to Cope with Great Anger

How can I cope with great anger I feel toward a person? How can I work and/or live with problematic people?

Short-term: **If someone really pisses you off, ask yourself the humanizing question, "Why would a reasonable, rational, decent person do what I saw, and what role did I play in it?"** One theory says the main mistake tends to be we assume only a personality (motivational) factor in others (the so-called "dispositional view"). They do it because they are bad. We don't see that the situation pushes them to do it. We do not make this mistake in ourselves (the so-called "attribution error"). (26)

Long-term: if you've found love or a good relationship, but you undergo a trauma, you could end up "coping" in a way that pushes love away. **Prioritize not only connection but also your own capacity to process emotions and stress.** If you're struggling, get a good therapist. Join a support group. Invest in a workshop. Take personal growth seriously so you are available for connection. (65)

The Three R's Method

Be Respectful, take an inteRest in the person, and take their Requirements into account (the three Rs). **Look for what you can learn from everyone.**

The Art of Living Alone, Should You Wish to Do So

Feelings of loneliness are toxic. People who are more isolated from others than they would like feel less happiness, experience a faster decrease in brain function, and live shorter lives than those who are not lonely. What matters is the quality of close relationships. (100)

What if I still will want to live alone?
Some are living alone without a spouse, and they can have a rich, meaningful, and satisfying retirement. Research has shown **the following factors contribute to a happy retirement for single retirees**:
— Good health
— Steady and adequate income
— Social support
— Emotional support
— Community involvement
— Personal hobbies
— Intellectual pursuits (31)

People who like themselves live a happy and successful retirement just as much when they are alone as when they were working. This applies to all retirees, married or single.

Solitude is not the same as loneliness. Some people are afraid to be alone because of fear of isolation, unhappiness, or negative self-assessment. Yet only by being alone a lot can they conquer loneliness. **It is only after you can establish a meaningful relationship with yourself that you can build strong, healthy, and lasting relationships with others.** When you master the art of solitude, you master yourself and life in general. Best of all, you no longer experience loneliness.

Approach to Make Friends at All Levels

☐ **Action step** - Sit down and think quietly:
- How many real **friends** do you have in your life **now**?
- What **wider circle of people** will you want to have? **Friends at all levels?** People who will broaden your thinking horizons, puncture your social bubble, give you honest feedback, inspire you to think about things, and try new things?
- Among your more distant social connections, who are the **people** you also care about **who bring you some value**?
- What **communities**? Professional and interest **associations**? **Clubs**? **Webinars**?
- What **new ways** will you start to become **connected to others**?
- What can you do today to **improve your communication skills**?

Add the new relevant steps, goals, and tasks to your list of goals.

5-Action-Steps Approach to Bring It All Together

Herminia Ibarra, professor of organizational behavior: "Networking is a lot like nutrition and fitness: We know what to do. The hard part is making it a top priority."

☐ **Action step**: What level of **technological proficiency** will you need to maintain your social plan, relationships, and fulfilment? What improvements in technology do you need? What will you do to get there? Whose help do you need? When will you learn it? Add the goals to your list of goals.

☐ **Action step**: Start **planning the rest of your life**.
Ask yourself: *What would this world look like if everyone behaved like me?*
Ask yourself: *Am I now who I want to be? Is the time they spend with me the best part of their day?* (Chester Elton)

Practice six ways to make friends.
Ask yourself: *Did I make a difference today?* Keep adding **goals from the social plan and relationships** to your already written goals. Don't forget family, friends, and medium and weak ties.
Try subjecting these goals to the criteria of **PVES**.[24]

☐ **Action step**: Think about life after work, and ask yourself these three questions:
— What can I do to continue making a **contribution**?
— In what can I find **meaning**?
— What will make me **happy**? (2)

---

24 Positive; Visualized; Exciting and Emotional - you really want it; unrealistic a little Scary. They will thus become motivating.

☐ **Action step**: Put a **meeting with yourself** on your calendar **once a month** and **review your goals, including the three questions** from the previous action step.

☐ **Action step**: Make your social environment audit and customize it accordingly.

☐ Homework: **Plan how you will complete your goals in terms of your social plan.**

In summary, creating great friends and learning how to enjoy yourself while alone are two of the most precious gifts you can give yourself.

This will contribute to your happy and fulfilled Third Act of life.

You will be able to do what you have planned for when you want, with whom you want, wherever you want, for as long as you want in your Third Act of life. Your retirement years will be the best time of your life.

Chapter 9: Your Lifestyle Plan

> "If the soul has food for study and learning, nothing is more delightful than an old age of leisure." Cicero

You may be asking yourself: *How do I want to live in retirement? What do I want to experience? What I'm going to need to do that? Who/what do I want to be dependent on or independent from?*

Do you have sufficient confidence in your own ability to live life without any guidance or interference from someone else?

Are you clear on the use of personal freedom, leisure, and change of life structure that you will gain in retirement?

By understanding the steps to build your emotional health lifestyle plan, possible approaches and techniques, and your attitude, you will have meaning for your fresh start prepared so you can live a happy and fulfilled retirement.

Your mission for this chapter — should you choose to accept it — is to create a new identity for your fresh start, a plan for spending your time by building a "portfolio" of activities, and learn emotional health techniques, so your new identity, not based on work, will make decades of your retirement a joy to look forward to and experience fully.

Imagine all the personal freedom, leisure, and change of life structure that you will gain in retirement. Also imagine seeing yourself as a new person with new desires and possibilities of how to live your new life. Possibly you will add another item to your meaning (= WHY) of retirement life, so you will make your retirement years the best time of your life.

After studying this chapter, you will discover:
— How to search for meaning (your WHY)[25] for your Third Act
— How to build your emotional health lifestyle plan
— The common but wrong way
— General steps for your emotional health
— How to create a new identity for your fresh start
— Some other tools you may want to use
— How to build your routines

---

25 Some may think of it as purpose, direction, mission, vision, dreams, desires, or wants. It is closely related to mind care, fulfilment, emotional health, which will be discussed in this chapter, too.

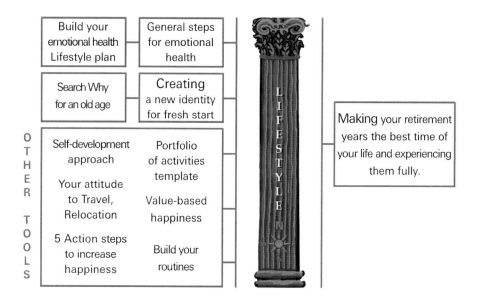

Henry David Thoreau: "If one advances confidently in the direction of his dreams, and endeavors to live the life which he has imagined, he will meet with a success unexpected in common hours."

Introduction

Tens of millions are heading toward retirement in the U.S. (baby boomers). They will have better health and live longer than their parents. All of them will face these questions: ***Do I want a reason to get up in the morning and be excited about the day ahead? Do I still want to make a difference in the world?*** Having a purpose motivates and energizes people in their retirement years. Identify a goal toward which you can strive. Striving for that goal brings meaning, satisfaction, and a sense of reward to retirement years. (68)

Two out of three retirees enter their Third Act having given little or no thought to the non-financial components of retirement life, only to discover that those "soft side" elements (mental, physical, social, spiritual) play a much larger role in retirement than the "hard-side" financial elements, where the major pre-retirement planning effort is normally focused. Unfortunately, this discovery often comes later than it should. Much of the early, prime-time Third Act is wasted because of this lack of non-financial planning. New retirees typically experience 1-5 years of a "retirement honeymoon" period, during which the mental, social, physical, and spiritual challenges emerge, which were never discussed or planned for in advance. Some common issues are loss of identity, divergent post-retirement interests between spouses, boredom due to lack of challenge and social engagement, depression and physical deterioration because of reduced activity and social interaction, and lacking a sense of purpose. (82)

A study of 83,000 Americans aged 65 and older published in *Preventing Chronic Disease*, a publication of the U.S. Center for Disease Control and Prevention, found that **being unemployed or retired was associated with the greatest risk of poor health**. (88)

A study of nearly half a million French people found that people who retired at 65 had about 15% lower risk of dementia than those who retired at 60 (even after taking other factors into account). (100)

Even if you manage to have friends to spend time with and live where you planned to, you might be missing a sense of purpose and meaning for your retirement life. **You will want to keep growing as an individual**, not remaining stagnant. (31)

You may think: *I am clear on my values and life meaning. Why should I care more about it in retirement?*

Many retirees end up depressed and hate retirement. Many experience a quick decline of mental and physical health thanks to idleness and feelings of uselessness. Therefore, one must stay active.

McArthur Foundation research indicated that keeping the brain active, engaged, and constantly learning helps to prolong its health and ability to function properly. Intellectual challenges can help get it in better shape than it has ever been.

Our minds can continue to grow and become gradually more fit with time in any age (neuroplasticity) if we want. Other research has shown that **people with high levels of intelligence and education tend to have lower rates of Alzheimer's disease** and age-related mental decline. (100)

Regardless of how old you are, there is always something intriguing to learn and the opportunity to do so.

Don Herold: "The brighter you are, the more you have to learn."

Laurence J. Peter: "The best intelligence test is what we do with our leisure."

Provided you are creative (anyone can develop this talent), you can discover outlets for self-expression that are more exciting and fulfilling than any of your past work-related accomplishments ever were. **The degree to which you can handle leisure will determine the overall quality of your Third Act.**

Cicero: "Leisure consists in all those virtuous activities by which a man grows morally, intellectually, and spiritually. It is that which makes a life worth living."

Nearly 92% of U.S. retirees say "having purpose is key to a successful retirement." Research also has shown that having a sense of purpose can actually reduce the risk of cognitive decline, cardiovascular disease, and depression and is essential to a healthy and satisfying retirement. (86)

Do you go to bed or get up in the morning feeling necessary? **Being necessary or useful or indispensable each day adds meaning to our lives.** Without it, what meaning does life have? It gets easier as we get older to become more necessary with our accumulated experiences and wisdom. **Being necessary can take any form.** (88)

I observe that aging often amplifies negative qualities in people. What will you do to prevent that from happening to you? How are you going to work on yourself?

Being productive with one's free time takes initiative and creativity, the two things most people have not developed.

Ask yourself: *How do I want to live? What do I want to experience? What am I going to need to do that? Who/what do I want to be dependent on or independent from?* Prepare about 10 years in advance.

Unknown: "I am currently under construction. Thank you for your patience."

It's about **mental health**, positive attitudes about life and the future, constant learning and curiosity about new knowledge, being able to cope with life's challenges, enjoying life, and being able to be grateful for it. It has a huge **impact on relationships. Mental health also impacts physical health and vice versa.** One without the other languishes.

If you are **grateful**, you can face hardships with courage and positivity. During the most difficult times, you may even find that it gives you strength and resilience that you were otherwise unaware of.

Limit the extent of negative information coming to you, namely from watching news (on TV or radio). Rather fill your mind every day with more positive information. This will give you a happier, more productive outlook on life in general and will help your body relax. The first and last things that go into your mind every day and every night should be positive, uplifting, happy, and peaceful. (59)

You may be asking, *What is the COVID-19 impact on this pillar?* The partial answer (at least for the U.S.) according to the Investments & Wealth Institute is retirees said they feel more optimistic than other Americans said they feel, despite the increased risk of getting the virus. Sixty-one percent say the pandemic has given them "more appreciation for what makes life meaningful." And 53% say they now have greater "empathy and compassion for people who are struggling in ways that [they are] not." (86) I have no data for other countries, but I believe the right approach will make you more optimistic, too.

The Common but Wrong Way

My friend Jim talked to one retired couple. They're very successful in their business. They've already passed the business onto someone else. But from Jim's observation, they're missing a big part of their own personal lives. He doesn't want to do anything; she wants to do too much. She has no direction but wants to do things. She's afraid that he's going to be not doing anything. They have some real, serious issues. She has an apartment in the city, and 15-20 minutes away they have their house. She lives in the city, and he lives at the house. It's not that they don't have a good marriage, but it's not a healthy marriage. She shared this with my friend, and he shared with her the Third Act concept. She does recognize that she doesn't have the Third Act down. All they're doing is scheduling time. She said, "I want to travel." He said, "And then what? What is it? Are you going to do nothing but travel for 10 years?" She said, "Well, no," he said, "Then what are you doing in between?" She said, "I don't know." She worked so hard in her second act to prepare for the Third Act for her and for her son. She's ahead of the curve more than most people, but she's so out of balance that she doesn't know what she's doing. She's ready now to enjoy the best part of her life, but she's very, very confused.

To be bored is to retire from life. Don't make the mistake of **making the couch, the fridge, and the TV your three best friends.** (31) This **contributes to poor mental and physical health**.[26] Symptoms associated with boredom, such as being unhappy, depressed, or lonely, can be more bothersome daily for retirees than physical symptoms. Just being busy, however, is not enough to avoid boredom. Even a favorite leisurely pursuit can lead to boredom if one spends too much time on it. (31)

---

26 The American Heart Association states: "Science has linked being inactive and sitting too much with higher risk of heart disease, type 2 diabetes, colon and lung cancers, and early death."

We've all seen friends, family members, acquaintances, or former workmates slip into role-less, goal-less lifestyles in the Third Act. Invariably, the results are an accelerated physical and/or mental decline. (82)

Ellen Parr: "The cure for boredom is curiosity. There is no cure for curiosity."

Finding Your WHY (Meaning) For Old Age

According to Martin Seligman, five important factors leading to more lasting satisfaction are Positive emotions, intense Engagement, good Relationships, a sense of Meaning, and Accomplishment (PERMA). (147).

You may be thinking, *I want to retire from work/my boss. Will this make me happy?*

It's important to **retire to something rather than away from something**. It is necessary to **look for meaning for your old age**, preferably something **active and independent of others**. (3) To be able to say to yourself (to quote Jirina Siklova, Czech sociologist), **"I can still do a lot, but I don't have to do almost anything. It is a phase of great freedom."**

Realize that you are no longer responsible for others. **You can do whatever you want.** You don't have to look at what others will say. You have time and freedom to find your real self, to become more than you have ever been, **to become the type of person you have always wanted to become**. The happiest people, even in "life after work," find a way to still **contribute to the world** and find contentment and meaning (their **WHY, something more than self**).

Viktor E. Frankl, *Man's Search for Meaning:* "Those who have a 'why' to live can bear with almost any 'how.'"

Buddha: "Your purpose in life is to find your purpose and give your whole heart and soul to it."

Many authors: "You are free to give life meaning,

whatever meaning you want to give it."

Many adopt generativity as a goal. We all want to check out having left a footprint of some sort. Generativity is one path for accomplishing that. We've all likely known those who have sustained a vibrant vitality and perhaps extended longevity through their commitment to volunteerism or other methods of generativity. (82)

Living a meaningful Third Act life has a direct positive impact on our health, level of happiness, and motivation.

Erik Erikson: "I am what survives me."

My meaning for my Third Act of life, after years of working, putting money aside, and gaining knowledge (my sense of purpose), is now to enjoy my life as much as I can and do the things I always wanted to do but never had enough resources (time, money) to do. I want to expand my experience and enrich myself. At the same time, I seek to give my knowledge, wisdom, and experience to other people to support them in having their Third Act be fulfilled, happy, and calm. I can achieve the same level of motivation and daily enthusiasm now as I once had in the corporate world.

Dan Sullivan: "Always make sure your future is bigger than your past in terms of what you are interested in and what your goals are."

Creating a New Identity for Your Fresh Start

Retirement should be a reorientation of living, a fresh start. We should rather call it a "self-actualization" or "self-realization." We are soaring to new heights, both outwardly and inwardly. (31)

You may be afraid: *When I stop working, I may have no purpose to live, and I may die in a couple of months/years. Can I prevent that?*

Many people are used to having work as part or all of their identity. In a fresh start, you must change some assumptions. **You do not need a work identity to be a complete person.** You got by without a work identity the first 20 years of your life. You can do it for another 20 years or longer (otherwise you deny yourself happiness and peace of mind).

Stacy Peralta: **"Be careful of falling in love with identity... If you are locked in, it will hold your future hostage."**

Marisa Murgatroyd: **"You are not your business. Keep that separation. You have your inherent values."**

Your retirement reward should be life that is at least as exciting and interesting as your work life was. **With a constructive use of your time, you can be happier than you ever were.**

Your essence is the feeling of being a **whole human person**, not based on any superficial identity (work-related, possessions, status, power, net worth, or other). **Your true self is based on more profound things**, such as creativity, kindness, passionate pursuits, generosity, love, joy, spontaneity, connectedness to others, sense of humor, peace of mind, inner happiness, and possibly spirituality. **A new identity based on these traits will make retirement a joy to experience. Retirement is the time to live in the manner you have always dreamed of living.** Reflect upon your values.

Discover what is important to you.

You probably want a **new title** to express to others what you do in life (but not calling yourself a retiree). Tell people you only **work when you want and only on projects that make an important difference in this world**.

As we get older, each of us is more valuable today than we were ten years ago because of our experiences and what we've learned. The world needs us more than it ever has. To withdraw into isolation — so common in retirement or following a major loss of any sort — is a disservice to self and to society. We can all be necessary to someone or something. (88)

Mark S. Walton: "Find a way to work for the sake of others, and you will step up."

If you believe in the power of affirmations, you can download and recite this one every morning (Affirmation for the new identity for fresh start.pdf):

> I am too prosperous to work long and hard hours. I have earned my prosperity and deserve the right to enjoy a creative and satisfying lifestyle. I am too spiritually evolved to have an identity based on my work, possessions, and net worth.
>
> Instead, I am able to fully use all the personal freedom, leisure, and the change of life structure. My new identity is based on more profound things, including my creativity, my generosity, my spontaneity, my sense of humour, my peace of mind, my passion for new experiences, my happiness, and my spirituality. I make my retirement years the best time of my life, and a joy to experience.

Affirmation for the new identity for fresh start

It's never too late to start designing a Third Act you will truly love.

Michael Altshuler: "The bad news is time flies. The good news is you're the pilot."

Steps to Build Your Emotional Health Lifestyle Plan

Don't rely on money alone in the pursuit of happiness. Don't rely on fate or other people to show you the way. **Find your own way. Otherwise, you will not achieve full contentment.** (31)

John Barrymore: "A man is not old until regrets take the place of dreams."

Listen to your inner values and decide what you really want from your Third Act, not what others want from you or what others are doing. **Use your own creativity and inner wisdom.** You have your own dreams and goals. Create a lifestyle that expresses who you are. **There is no right way. There is only your way.**

Reintegrate yourself. (82)

Martha Washington: "The greater part of our happiness or misery depends on our dispositions and not our circumstances."

Research shows that most of the things people assume will make them happier, like money, beauty, and social status, don't matter much in the long run. (31)

☐ Homework: Take notes while reading. You will decide which steps you want to take in terms of your retirement lifestyle, mind care, fulfilment, and purpose, and add tasks/goals to your list of goals.

Decide which steps you want to make an entry for in your calendar.

For some steps, you may want to place a sticky note onto your refrigerator.

Don't exaggerate your relationship to/influence of your boss during your career. (Where will they be in 5 years, right?)

Plan for spending your time:

How long do you want to work? In what form? (Employment, sole trader, company owner. Full-time/part-time/alternate between full-time projects and "short-term pensions"/move from full-time to part-time employment or self-employed before stopping work altogether.)

Maybe you no longer want to work for money, prestige, or status but perhaps **to do good and be helpful**.

Think about your contribution. Do you want to remain in the memory of others, **leave a mark**, realize what you are blessed with, contribute positively to the world, leave a legacy, or look for how to help others? This is similar to what parents, friends, mentors, teachers, authors of books, etc. have done to help you.

John C. Maxwell: "You will never change your life until you change something you do daily. The secret of your success is found in your daily routine."

Aristotle: "We are what we do repeatedly."

There is a **need for new structure and routines**. **Stress** in retirement can come **from the lack of predictability, control, and social contact** — all formerly provided by a job. (31) A job also provided us a sense of self-worth, status, achievement, recognition, power, growth, meaning, purpose, satisfaction, friendship, and challenge. I believe jobs provide us with the means for satisfying (at least) three important needs: **Purpose, Community, and Structure. We must now find new ways that will provide** fulfillment of **these needs**. You may **start with identifying** which of these abovementioned (intangible, non-financial) **benefits work has provided you**. **Then think of** the types of **interests and leisure activities** that can **bring you** these benefits and rewards. This and previous chapters should help you in finding **purpose, community, and friends**. Let us speak of the **structure** here.

At the beginning, the loss of work-related structures and routines feels great. But most people like **at least some structure and routine**, as they bring comfort. Rigid people are not able to use the personal freedom to do what they want in retirement, and they withdraw from society, fall to desperation, and their mental and physical capabilities rapidly deteriorate. For **independently minded and self-motivated people**, the loss of structure will be a blessing. They **will enjoy** their **freedom and create new** routines, especially if they have created a driving purpose in life. For example, for me the new routines combine regular exercising, walking, cycling, cross-country skiing, supporting the family, reading, writing this book and course, chatting with friends, coaching, and mentoring.

Deepak Chopra: "Daily routines are important for retarding the aging process."

Use your creativity to design your routines. We will have a special chapter on routines later. Routine is good to a certain degree. We all need some, but we can admit the **importance of being spontaneous** for avoiding boredom and deep ruts. Be spontaneous as children are at least once a week. Give yourself permission to **try something new**, to do something impulsive. Instead of having your rational mind reject the idea as silly, allow more chance in your life.

Retirement as a fresh start allows you great opportunity to get away from routines. **Have unstructured time every day. Vary your weekends.**

Be able to be different. It has two aspects: **be different from the way you have always been. And** be different **from the way others are**.

Bad Times, Good Deeds, and Connection with People

In a time of crisis, **everything bad, any problem, can be turned into a gift. It's always possible.** It may sound like a cliché, but in my view, it is at least an opportunity to appreciate what we have (in comparison to most people in other continents/countries). Factual well-being is not a given. Feel gratitude and humility. And moreover, you can always find and commit to an **inspiring action** that you **wouldn't have done without the bad event**. (20)

The instruction is simple: **Start with an activity in**

which you find meaning. It sounds trivial, but to put it as Nietzsche would: Life is suffering. And survival depends on finding meaning in that suffering. For example, as one American program demonstrated, seniors there were suddenly happier and felt less lonely when they could tutor and care for children in nearby elementary schools. I, for example, became a coach and wrote this book.

Do good deeds. For example, donate money to charity or volunteer to read stories to children or seniors online. As research has documented, doing good helped people feel more connected to others, and they were happier overall. And, it was more beneficial when people **alternated between different types of good deeds**. Once we get into the habit of doing something regularly, it feels natural. (6)

This **greater connection with other people** is basic advice for a good life. As a study spanning more than 80 years has shown, good relationships are far more important for a happy and healthy life than, for example, the level of wealth or the quality of our genes. (148) The simple advice is: Create a **web of relationships around you** that will act as a **psychological safety net** in times of need.

If you want to be happier in the coming months, try **showing more gratitude**, too. One study published in the journal *Personality and Individual Differences* concluded **grateful people experience less pain and take more care of themselves**, often extending their lives. For example, try writing a thank-you note to someone. And you don't even have to send it. Psychologists have found that even without sending it, the letter writer's feelings of gratitude increased significantly and continued for another three months. (6)

Write down the things for which you feel gratitude. Tell people you appreciate them. Gratitude sparks the dopamine and serotonin that will make you feel better, improve your sleep, and help you maintain a more positive outlook. Avoid comparing yourself with other people. Appreciate what you have and share your gratitude with others. (37)

Marcus Aurelius: "Do not dream of possession of what

you do not have. Rather reflect on the greatest blessings in what you do have, and on their account remind yourself how much they would have been missed if they were not there."

Another piece of advice: **Focus on the present.** One of the biggest psychological impacts of the pandemic is that it has brought a huge degree of uncertainty about the future. Meanwhile, psychologists working with patients who had suffered serious injuries or were chronically ill noticed that these people coped with the stress of an unknown future by living day to day. It doesn't mean that they have resigned to a future life. They just saw the road to it as **a series of obstacles to be overcome**, one by one, day by day. (6)

Victory lies close behind defeat.

Be curious, too, and don't be afraid to **marvel at the small beauties the world brings**. It sounds like a cliché, but a study published in Emotion magazine shows that it works. (6)

As the popular comedian George Carlin once wisely said, "Life should not be measured by the number of breaths we take but by the number of moments that take our breath away." In pandemic times, this sentence might sound like dark humor, but believe me. You can experience plenty of such positive moments every day. **Just look around you.**

Self-Development Approach

Lifelong learning and self-development are possible at any age ("neuroplasticity"). **Choose what information to let in.** (Limit the news.) **Choose the people around you** — associate with inspiring and positive people. What you talk about becomes your world.

Prepare for the unexpected by engaging in **continuous learning and network building**. On the surface, taking time from other to-dos to learn new things may seem difficult. But it benefits you in the long run to keep your skills up to date. You may want to read blogs, books, and white papers; listen to podcasts or audiobooks; take online classes, watch videos, or attend conferences and seminars; follow thought leaders on social media; or even go back to school to earn a formal degree in a new area. Put learning time on your calendar. (75)

You can take college courses for the satisfaction and enjoyment of it. Lifelong learning is for those who know they are not retiring from life — just from a job. Five hundred thousand seniors are enrolled nationally in colleges and universities in the U.S., many of them in non-degree courses.

Modern Elder Academy: "Success is not about winning. Success is about learning."

It all boils down to an inner change. Stephen R. Covey speaks about circles of influence and how we should start from the inside out. That's the first habit of Highly Successful People. **We can change anything within, and good things will eventually emerge.** (128)

The good news: **Our brains can make new connections** between neurons (neuroplasticity) **throughout our lives**, i.e., learn! The potentially worse news: Our brain is constantly changing depending on how we use it.

Portfolio of Activities and Hobbies Template

Maybe you think, *I know what hobbies I will spend time with. Why should I care about adding more for retirement?*

Imagine retiring and suddenly dropping 8-10 hours a day. How do you fill them? Starting new hobbies is hard enough. Expanding existing hobbies is easier. Try to think about and cultivate them as far in advance as possible. Ideas: sports, gardening, travel, singing, playing a musical instrument(s), writing, cooking, cottage, technology (PC, audio/video), coaching/mentoring, investing in self-development, and so on. We will say more in the next action step.

Action Step

For this and subsequent action steps you may want to download the template for you to fill in Possible Activities in Retirement.xlsx

After you fill the template in, include it in your list of goals and action steps you want to take for the Third Act.

☐ **What "portfolio" of hobbies and activities will you compile?**

Check if your activities meet the criteria from Value-Based-Happiness Method chapter -see later. Has the pandemic offered you an opportunity to prepare for the next phase of your life?

Be passionate, not passive.

General Steps for Emotional Health (Using Positive Intelligence)

Minimize thoughts of illnesses, Covid, or war. **Think positive.**

Use the experience you've gained over the years to step back, be above it all, and adopt the attitude of a sage.

Enjoy life, even the status of your health. (It's good it is what it is and not worse). **Happiness is a matter of our choice.** It can be achieved, it takes effort, and it pays off.

It is all too easy to fall into the trap of thinking that practically everyone else has a much easier and happier life than you do. One of the most important steps to enjoy life to the fullest is an absence of envy of others. You cannot be both envious and happy. (31)

Don't compare yourself to anyone else. Only compare yourself to how you used to be some time ago and how you have progressed.

Try an approach from positive psychology: PERMA. Ask yourself these questions to reveal and realize your PERMA level. Answer each question on a scale from 1 (worst)

to 10 (best), or fill in the online test of M. Seligman of Penn University.
(https://www.authentichappiness.sas.upenn.edu/questionnaires/perma)

- **P**(positive emotions): Do you have mostly positive emotions in your life? Experience them in the moment.
- **E**(engagement): Do you experience flow states when you are completely emersed in an activity you enjoy? How often?
- **R**(relationships): Are your relationships (with loved ones, in the workplace, and with friends) fulfilling and positive?
- **M**(meaning): Have you found a purpose in life that exceeds you?
- **A**(accomplishment, achievement): Are you successful in fulfilling your life goals? In improving yourself?

Be aware of this concept and keep doing mindful decisions that move you closer to 10 in each part.

Concrete Steps to Build Your Emotional Health Lifestyle Plan

Create and maintain your **personal vision**. A good guide, for example, can be Peter Ludwig's process from his book *The End of Procrastination*. (73). A good coach can help you with that, too.

Assess which of the following activities apply to you (use the template provided earlier):

Learn **mindfulness** and use it during the day.

Positive Visualization - mindfulness on something I wish for. (11)

Humor - the fullness of life. Watch out for petty things that can make it disappear.

Participate.

Family.

Travel, mountains - appropriate to your abilities, interests, and personal risk level.

Good and **healthy food**, wine.

House, informed gardening or farming. A modern garden may now contain plants for health and healing. Do you have a garden? When will you get one?

Friends.

Social anchorage. Horizontal relationships (people close to your age) are at least as important as vertical ones. Carefully seek and cultivate **peer friendships**.

Meet new people.

Golf, **sport**.

Hobbies. It's hard but possible to find new hobbies in retirement.

Combine hobbies with your social life.

Collect experiences and make the most of them, **imagining them as vividly as possible a long time beforehand, being prepared for minor disappointments during the event, then remembering and sharing them for as long as possible with others and friends**.

Clubs or **interest groups**.

Consider getting a pet.

Visit spa.

Read.

Volunteer, do charity work, help foundations. **Passing on acquired knowledge** can lead to great satisfaction, as it can give life great meaning.

Train others, lecture, promote active discussion.

Consider school courses and webinars. **Keep learning** (prevention against Alzheimer's disease). Admit that it's **possible at any age** and start it. The brain can do it and likes it very much. Nothing keeps your mind in shape as much as learning.

Art. Perceive art, be influenced by art, lighten up, and try your own experiments. Be active and creative.

Music, singing.

Coaching.

Make up your own topics using the template provided.

Kerry Patterson: "The secret of happiness lies not in the act of creating joy. The secret of happiness lies in recognizing joy when it comes."

You may want to download a basic list: 10 Simple Habits to Live Longer and Better.pdf

Your Attitude about Travel & a Travel Planning Checklist

Traveling is a great pleasure and adventure in retirement. It can be part of your vision and make your retirement very fulfilling. You may want to get to know new people, history, customs, other views of retirement and life in general, the local geography, or nature. You can learn something new everywhere and from everyone. You will get new perspectives on life and new horizons. You will realize what a good life you are living and what good retirement brings you. Travel should be part of your time in retirement. (31)

Decide whether or how much of your savings you want to leave to your children and **what you will spend on travel**, if your health allows you to travel.

Be positive and plan your trip. You can download and fill in the Travel Preparation Checklist.pdf

Think about who you want to travel with. You can ask friends or acquaintances or use the internet to find suitable company. There are many such web services in most countries.

Your Attitude toward Relocating for Retirement

In both the U.S. and Western Europe, **many retirees** choose to **relocate temporarily or permanently within their own country, continent, or elsewhere on earth**. This may be for financial reasons. They may want a different climate (warmer or more snow), nice and clean nature, forests, mountains, lakes or the ocean, different company, culture, comfort, new excitement, or, on the contrary, proximity to children and grandchildren. Keep in mind the availability of health/medical care, transportation, infrastructure, library, taxes, etc. And be sure to go there several times beforehand for a holiday at different times of the year.

Action Step - Possible Activities in Your Retirement Planning Blueprint

☐ **Action step**: Download Possible Activities in Retirement.xlsx. You will add activities according to your general steps for emotional health, travel, and relocating for retirement preferences.

Fill in your opinions on suitability for you based on these criteria:
1. Turns me on now
2. Has turned me on in the past
3. Is a new activity that I would consider doing
4. Does not interest me at all

Choose and do something. One step in the right direction will be worth 100 years of thinking about it.

☐ Homework: Go back to your list of goals and enhance your action steps. Print it. Keep coming back to it. It's a long-term tool. Add or delete items as your life situation changes.

Linking Your Social Plan to Your Strategy

Mission = your big WHY(s), the will to have **meaning or direction**, not to accept social stereotypes. **The will to go against the tide.** (4)

People want to pursue things that have **real meaning**. No one wants to become a has-been in the sense of "Weren't you an important person?" They want to have real meaning in the world. (2)

In the Third Act, **there is a need for stimuli**, the need for **recognition**, the need for **structure**. It means to live in a world of people and not be pushed back. (4)

Marshall Goldsmith on **happiness**: "Everyone wants that. It cannot be bought. It **must be lived**. On a deeper level, it cannot be separated from **meaning and contribution** — it comes from them." (2)

Sit down and think quietly: *What is my relation to something higher?* It's a connection to my **values**, my **identity** (who I am, what I would ideally call myself), the **deeper meaning** of my actions, my direction, and my life. *What do I want as my legacy?* **How do I want others to remember me?** You may want to include your relation to faith or spirituality. Overall, it's something you can **lean on in times of difficulty** to help you **make the right decision**.

Finding Meaning for Your Fresh Start

People who have a purpose tend to live 7-10 years longer and have a more fulfilling and happier life. (52)

We all have different needs. Some seek entertainment. Ernie J. Zelinski believes **people with higher education** who have had responsible and fulfilling careers seek enrichment. They require some level of **risk, challenge, meaning, and accomplishment**. They seek **more purpose, excitement, and adventure**. (31) I agree that the more people are satisfied with the **purpose and meaning** of their lives, the **easier they feel their Third Act is**. Their personal and emotional life is greatly enhanced. **An overriding purpose is a great antidote for depression.** You get to feel useful, committed, and productive. And purpose can only be found from within. Find out who you really are. If you don't have your purpose yet, take time to explore your deeper self (possibly with help of a coach).

Many people have been focused on material possessions, status, competition, and consumption. They have worked hard and earned a lot of money. But they have

forgotten who they will be, or are now in their Third Act and have forgotten what they deeply care about, what really turns them on. They have **enough money to do what they want but are not quite sure what that is**.

If you do not have your meaning for retirement, keep looking and exploring. If you don't have your meaning yet, don't despair. Don't panic. Discovering it is a nice activity at an age when you have already done some work and there is something to discover in your history. Devote enough time and effort to self-discovery.

Mark Twain: "The two most important days of your life: the day you were born and the day you find out why."

If seniors see meaning in life, they are more likely to avoid a lot of illnesses, from mild cognitive impairment and Alzheimer's disease to disability, heart attack, or stroke, and are more likely to live to a higher age than people without such a strong inner drive. (100)

Why meaning has such power can be logically justified. The mission goes hand in hand with the motivation to stay physically active and take better care of ourselves, which allows us to better manage stress and decrease dangerous inflammation. (100)

The feeling of life fulfillment also goes with optimism. The 2018 Global Council on Brain Health report ranks optimism as an important element of well-being. This also includes self-acceptance, vitality, and positive relationships. (149)

How to discover your meaning? Try to search in the past. You need to understand what is unique in your life story. You need to go through your values and passions and extract your strengths. Some people formulate their mission quickly; for others it takes a few years. Some have prepared their Third Act meaning in advance and can possibly only update it. Some have not prepared at all and must reinvent completely. When you discover your mission, you will understand it is the mission that makes you who you really are as a retiree. It is like an umbrella spreads over everything.

Look for continuity of meaning. Discover what you are passionate about. Do so several years in advance. Think of how you can still contribute, be valued, and feel worthwhile.

In case you are having difficulty discovering an important purpose in life, you might welcome the list of **questions to ask yourself**. (See the template: Some questions to ask yourself if having difficulty discovering an important purpose in life.pdf.)

Your meaning (WHY) should ideally consist of three parts:
1. Big Altruistic Why — simple purpose behind your retirement; the reason you want to retire
2. Big Intrinsic (inherent, essential) Why — sense of joy, purpose, and fulfillment you feel every day
3. Big Selfish Why — what retirement allows you to do, be, have, or receive (that you couldn't before); your selfish reason for retirement.
    (Based on Marisa Murgatroyd (36))

Whatever you choose, **do something** and be clear about your goal: **You are no longer doing it for prestige, status, competition**, or **material pursuits**. You don't need to be admired. You are doing it **for yourself**, for your soul. It makes sense to you. Or you're doing it for a noble cause (preferably both).

Regardless of how much you want to immerse yourself in your major purpose or your most passionate pursuit in life, you should also learn to enjoy other leisure activities. The quality of each of your retirement days should be evaluated, at least in part, by how much you **relaxed, laughed, and played**. (31)

In my opinion, don't bet on a single activity. **Look for a balance of activities.** Develop a set of activities that are worth pursuing. Research has confirmed that **people with many interests live not only the happiest lives but the longest, too.** (31)

Live your later life actively, meaningfully, and enjoy it.
Happy people are the players. Unhappy people are the spectators.

How happy you will be in retirement will depend on whether you are willing to be happy.

Seneca: "Life is long if it is full."

Modern Elder Academy: "The challenge of humanity is that living a long time does not guarantee wisdom. Age does not guarantee growth."

Value-Based Happiness Method

Eckhart Tolle: "The primary cause of unhappiness is never the situation but thought about it. Be aware of the thoughts you are thinking. Separate them from the situation, which is always neutral. It is as it is." (96)

In contrast to feel-good happiness (like watching TV), **value-based happiness** comes from meaningful activities that **serve some higher purpose** than just plain pleasure. This happiness **stems from attaining a sense of satisfaction**. Satisfaction is attained from fulfilling **some deeper purpose in tune with our values**. The activities contributing to value-based happiness are not normally ruled by the law of diminishing returns. And if they are, the satisfaction lasts a lot longer in comparison to feel-good ones. (14), (31)

Passive activities are typified by no real challenge, no overriding purpose, monotony, and lack of novelty. They are predictable, safe, and provide us security and safety along with pleasure, but (contrary to popular belief) we get no long-term satisfaction and self-fulfillment from them. Our passive activities must be complemented by active ones.

For some people, the **nature of leisure activities must change** when they retire. Jobs have provided them with challenges, accomplishment, and satisfaction. Their new leisure activities should provide this now as well as **challenge their mental and physical abilities**. Leisure activities should be **creative, challenging, and constructive**.

We get the most satisfaction from leisure activities that are more challenging and require high levels of intellectual energy. A leisure pursuit will be **truly satisfying if it meets all or most of the following eight criteria**:

1. You have a genuine interest in it.

2.   It is challenging.
3.   There is some sense of accomplishment associated
       with completing only a portion of it.
4.   It has many aspects to it, so it doesn't become boring.
5.   It helps you develop some skill.
6.   You can get so immersed in it that you lose a sense of
       time (state called "flow"[27]).
7.   It provides you with a sense of self-development.
8.   It doesn't cost too much.

Another method in identifying your values to find your meaning you may want to use (and possibly deliberately reprioritize for your Third Act of life) is working to consciously know what your most important values are and using them to see the bigger picture and make more conscious choices. Credit goes to Lubna Samara, Higher Will (70)

1.   Download the template List of Values.pdf.
2.   Choose around 25 of the values that speak to you.
3.   Group them all so that similar values will be under one
       heading.
4.   Keep doing this until you have three to five value
       headings that you're not able to group together.
5.   Think back to periods in your life where you may have
       had tricky situations and see if you're able to prioritize
       the four values you have. If you're not able to, that's
       OK.
6.   These will be the most important values for you, possibly
       during the whole of your life, but certainly for this period
       of your journey.

This exercise will bring you an awareness. In your real life, you may have shown different behaviors (for whatever reason), causing massive stress for you. We all want to love and respect ourselves. The Third Act gives you a chance to get rid of these reasons and pressures and live according to your values (and passions, experience, knowledge, and abilities).

There was a lady providing first aid to people camping

---

27 Concept described by Mihaly Csikszentmihalyi

out in the woods who got stuck using this as a hobby in her second act of life. When retired, she created online courses on simple first aid procedures, which later turned into a very successful business.

The Third Act is also related to another life transformation as you cut through your own ambitions. The dark forest, which has begun to loom on the far edge of your life, makes you realize what a precious gift life really is, and the most precious thing of all is the time you have left in it. This can be liberating. **Life makes sense**, and not as a list of accomplishments. Your day has come to late afternoon. The road disappears into the woods. But it's your path, and you can walk it as you want. (69)

If You Don't Want to Retire and Want a Fulfilling Career to 80 and Beyond

What if I want to continue working (maybe even to 80 and beyond)?

People who work long into retirement:
— see continuing to work as a pleasure
— lead a healthy life in terms of healthy eating, exercise, and mindfulness
— enjoy challenges, have a purpose in life, and learn from their work
— stave off mental decline through being busy
— know that successful aging is linked to resilience
— listen to classical music
— manage their stress
— find meaning as wisdom workers. Some cognitive qualities, such as pattern recognition, emotional intelligence, and learning can improve until very late in life
— take care of grandchildren
— reinvent their careers, often influencing younger generations
— learn, mentor, or coach

- know that part of wisdom is knowing yourself
- are open to new ideas, are curious. Such people move from trying to be interesting to being interested. (24)

Having enjoyable work while also having more leisure time is a great way to enjoy life. A fun job may end up being your true calling in life. Separate the meaning of a job from its normal trappings. (31) Disassociate yourself from how much money the job will pay, from the status and prestige you can attain, and from what others think about the job. You and only you must decide what is meaningful to you in a retirement career, what gives you satisfaction and enjoyment. You can also experiment with short-term or part-time jobs.

Start a lifestyle business. It has three components: a level of income you desire, time freedom (work when you want, as much as you want), and location independence. According to a U.S. Bureau of Labor Statistics report, the self-employment rate among workers 65 and older (who don't incorporate) is the highest of any age group in America: 15.5%. In sharp contrast, it's 4.1% for ages 25 to 34. (82)

The legendary cellist Pablo Casals was asked why he continued to practice at age 90. "Because I think I'm making progress," he replied.

Action Step - Positive Retirement Mood Phrases

☐ Choose phrases that resonate with you:
- I am wiser and can share that.
- I have more time to myself to study to know my inner resources.
- Life is wonderful in itself; I can constantly experience joy and pleasure.
- I can stop worrying about the past, find peace and serenity, and live and leave with grace and charm.
- I no longer care what others think of me.

Action Step - Mini-retirements, Pre-retirements, Semi-retirements, or Sabbaticals

☐ **Consider trying mini-retirements, pre-retirements, semi-retirements, or sabbaticals** as mental preparation for your Third Act. For example, as a contractor project manager, I sometimes worked intensively then not at all for a few months. As another example, an employee can divide a single working lifetime into several sections (say 15 years). In between sections, they take a few months break where they rest, get their health in order, educate themselves, and devote time and effort to themselves (for instance, think well about the tasks from this book). After that, they completely change their job and maybe even the field. Of course, you must **start as soon as possible.** Later, you can think about a semiretirement.

5-Action-Steps Approach to Increase Happiness

Knowledge is not power. Applied knowledge is power.

☐ **Action step:** What would I like my life and me to be like in the first five years (of my Third Act)?
(Based on (161)).

☐ **Action step:** Imagine what **I want people to say about me when I die**.

☐ **Action step: Reflection of the day**: Every day (for just a few minutes) write down:
— **What have I learned today?**
— **What made me happy?**
— **Whom did I help?**

— **Did I do my best today to be happy? To find meaning? To build positive relationships?** To be fully engaged? (And if not, what will I do? When?)

Annie Gottlier: "When some things go wrong, take a moment to be thankful for the many things that are going right."

Tool: **daily gratitude journal**.[28]   Write down:
— Three things I'm thankful for
— To whom I am grateful
— Visit them and thank them.
— Write a handwritten letter expressing gratitude (a powerful tool)
— Write an email expressing gratitude
— Say a simple thank you (perhaps to your loved ones).

Silence the negative. Try not to complain. **Never complain, never explain.**

Stop reading right now, grab a pen and paper, and write down five things that you are grateful for. Go ahead. I'll wait.

---

28 Writing down what you're grateful for is a powerful way to anchor that state of mind into your beingness. Researcher Robert Emmons confirmed with his research that after ten weeks, participants in the gratitude condition felt better about their lives as a whole and were more optimistic. Participants were over 25% happier, spent more time exercising, and reported fewer health complaints than those in the control group.

Not that tough, was it? We can always find something to be grateful for, but it seems we don't look for it, generally.

Add this step to your daily routines.[29]

Tony Robbins: "Most people are wired for stress. They're wired for frustration. They are wired for feeling lonely with a highway to p***ed off and a dirt road to happiness."

The two fears that mess us up are anger and fear, but we can't be angry or fearful and grateful at the same time.

Gilbert K. Chesterton: "I would maintain that thanks are the highest form of thought, and that gratitude is happiness doubled by wonder."

☐ **Action step: Imagine someone calling you every day and asking you the reflection of the day questions above.** Or ask yourself what questions you want them to ask you. You can ask someone to call you every day. Or you can ask someone to listen to your answers if you have the courage.

☐ **Action step**: Go back to your list of goals. Do you need to add any? Ask yourself every day: *Did I do my best today to set my goals? Did I make progress toward meeting them? Do I want to cross out some of the goals?*

Live the life you love; love the life you live.

Eat well, live well, think well!

Become the CEO of your life.

---

29 If you want to know more on gratitude, including another gratitude practice, you may want to listen to: https://www.youtube.com/watch?v=KVjfFN-89qvQ&t=258s

Visit **www.livingyourbestthirdact.com**. You will find free templates, exercises, checklists, outlines, work-sheets, and physical action plans there.

 THIRD ACT
RESOURCES

Chapter 10: Build Your Routines

It's very easy to slide away from your plans. It takes 66 days to firmly embed a good habit. (150). Other research on habit formation shows that the entire process can take 18 to 254 days (153). Anyhow, it won't happen without a disciplined, scheduled approach.

Bar Franek: "Spend your most valuable time on your most valuable activities, and you'll change the trajectory of your life."

Aytekin Tank: "The more systems we put in place, the less we find ourselves procrastinating."

James Clear: "Creating the right environment is as important as a strong will."

James Clear: "Don't form perfect habits. Form good enough habits."

Weekly Routines

Will Durrant: "We are what we repeatedly do. Excellence, then, is not an act, but a habit."

Matthew Emmorey: "You do not rise to the level of your goals. You fall to the level of your systems."

☐ **Action step**: The three things you take for granted. Ask yourself:

What is good in my life? What relationships, health status, successes, behaviors, or situations do I really enjoy and would not want to be without? What do I take for granted and not appreciate enough?

_____

_____

_____

_____

Increase your awareness about what's good in your life and allow yourself to feel it fully.

☐ **Action step**: **Imagine achieving the goals** you have set for yourself. Think about mini rewards for meeting the deadlines.

☐ **Action step**: **Plan other events into your calendar.** (This will increase the probability of reaching your goal by 1000%). **Don't say it's your priority unless you make room for it in your calendar.** Put reminders of the events **into your calendar** (for example, on your mobile phone) as a repeating item, every day or every week. Put **stickers on the fridge** or on the mirror.

☐ **Action step**: Plan basic endurance training (cyclical movement, such as running, a quick walk, swimming) 45 minutes, 3 times a week. Get your heartbeat up to 100-150 bpm (sweating but able to speak). Plan VO2 max training, where your heartbeat gets up to 150-160 bpm, once a week. Do strength training 1-2 times a week and active and passive regeneration 1-2 times a week. No excuses.

☐ **Action step**: You have your goals written. Now identify two actions: **"Uncomfortable actions challenge"** — **one** action you will start **immediately and one** action you will start **within one week** from now.

To achieve a long-term effect, you need to do uncomfortable things.

☐ **Action step**: Ask every week: ***Did I do my best to set my goals?*** *To move on to fulfill them?* Put a reminder into your calendar.

☐ **Action step**: Review your written goals every week. Add regular dates to the calendar to **revise your goals and refine your plans**. Don't lose sight of your long-term goals. It's about preparing for your retirement. Have the courage and discipline to do it.
Ask yourself: *What have I already accomplished in the past? Where did I move myself? Where do I want to move to next? What new goals do I want to add? What goals do I have to achieve in the next week to consider it a successful week?*

☐ **Action step**: **What helped you** meet your goals? **What prevents you?**

☐ **Action step**: What do you want to **praise yourself** for in the past period? **Whom** do you want **to thank**? Thank them. Tell them. Write to them.

☐ **Action step: Identify the people whose help and cooperation you will need** to achieve your goals. How can you attain their cooperation? What will they get out of it?

Remember, you need to be flexible but consistent. If you deviate from the program now and then, don't beat yourself up and just get back to it. Remember your written goals that motivate you a lot.

Daily Routines

Hal Elrod: "Repetition can be boring or tedious, which is why so few people ever master anything."

☐ **Action step**:
— Morning (or evening) gratitude ritual: Think for a few minutes about three things you're grateful about. Feel it in your heart. (You already know what you focus on

will expand, attracting more things you can be grateful for).

— You may want to write a gratitude journal, write gratitude mail, or do a gratitude visit.
— What have I learned today?
— What pleased me?
— Whom have I helped?
— What things will I ensure get done by the end of today, no matter what?
— Create your own little "blue zone" at home (Tips: morning meditation, regular relaxing moments during the day, sleep after lunch, techniques to manage acute stress). To what extent do I have my daily natural resilience system in place?
— Work on relationships every day just like you did in the office.
— How could you improve a relationship today? Figure out one thing and do it.
— Build your sleep routine. Try to go to bed around the same time each day. Build your dietary routines. Build your financial and social routines. Identify the most important task every day and complete it. Ask yourself: Which one activity would add the most value to my goals? Put a reminder in your calendar.
— Anticipate what obstacles may prevent you, even before you begin. And get ready for them.[30]

Establish what you will follow regularly, always, no matter what.

Build on your daily routines and transform them into a sustainable long-term lifestyle.

---

30 Define the obstacles you will have to overcome to achieve your goal. Identify the main constraints that are currently preventing you from achiev-ing your goal. Eighty percent of the reasons why you are not achieving your goals are within your control. They stem from a lack of certain skills or abil-ities that you can usually control. Only twenty percent of the obstacles or difficulties that prevent you from achieving your goals are not influenced by you but by other people or circumstances.(99)

Monthly Routines

Look back on what you have achieved. Enjoy it. Celebrate. It will give you encouragement. Your brain will calculate what is needed to repeat the actions.

Put a meeting with yourself into your calendar once a month and review your goals.

Is your path OK? Is there anything needing to be optimized?

☐ **Action step**: Review your spending at least one hour each month to continually find ways to save at least 15% of your annual income. (One significant difference between the wealthy and non-wealthy is that wealthy families spend twice as much time analyzing and planning their spending than non-wealthy families do). Then, as you earn more, keep your spending the same to gradually increase your savings rate from 15% to 20%, which is the average savings rate of millionaires in the wealth study. (160).

☐ **Action step**: Which goals will I add to my weekly routines from the following categories:
— Move more, exercise
— Learning, acquiring new knowledge
— Good sleep routines/rituals
— Proper dieting
— Socializing more

☐ **Action step**: **What will you regret** in many years not doing today? Add it to your goals while it can still be solved.

☐ **Action step**: **What** did the fulfillment or non-fulfillment of your goals **tell you about yourself**?

☐ **Action step**: Think from time to time: What is your next phase of life? What is your next move? Who do you need to consult with?

- What is one bad habit that, were you to quit it forever, would have the most significant impact more than any other change?
- What one habit will you replace this old bad habit with?
- What is one skill you can sharpen that will propel you quickly toward your goals?
- Who is one person who could help you accelerate your progress to what you want the most? How will you hook up with them or someone like them?

You may want to use Glad-Sad-Mad technique:
- Glad = what makes you happy. Do not neglect this step. Continue these actions.
- Sad = what did not please you. Acknowledge your mistakes.
- Mad = what drives you crazy, and what will you do with it?

Quarterly Routine

Where in your life right now might defining your fears be more important than defining your goals? Do a fear-setting routine (template Premeditatio malorum.pdf). Put your fears under scrutiny. It can make a lot of the hard choices easier.

Changing Old Routines

You may wonder: **What troubles will I encounter when changing my routines?**

Habits are very efficient. They require little energy and conscious work by our brains. It is beneficial to have them available where they work well.

But how do we deal with old habits that do not work well anymore or harm us? We can stop them through awareness. It's impractical to try to "erase" them. The most

successful strategy is to **replace them**.
1. Recognize the routine (an established pattern of behavior)
2. Experiment with different rewards
3. Recognize the trigger (what starts this pattern of behavior)
4. Have a plan (what to do when the trigger occurs)

Homework: Regularly check the lifestyle you lead. If you want, you can ask yourself the questions from the Lifestyle Checklist.pdf now and then once a year to check that you are on the road to a healthy, happy, and wealthy retirement. Answer honestly. **Be sure that your life choices are truly yours.** Don't pay attention to what other people do. Be yourself. Go to your list of goals and enhance your action steps.

Chapter 11:
Retirement Planning Is a Project

Congratulations on completing the entire book! I trust that you understand its importance and are confident that achieving the goals you have planned is within your power.

All the pillars we have gone through are actually projects. You are both the customer and sponsor/investor of these projects. And as in any project: Always begin by defining what exactly the project involves and **what is to be achieved**. Meaning is the root of achievement. We have learned how to create meaning, set goals, and follow a plan to achieve them. You have put a lot of effort into it. Now **follow your plans**. Go after your goals. Have them written down. Be **aware** of what can prevent you from achieving your goals. Be **adaptable**, flexible to changes in life conditions. Bring in experts as necessary. Go regularly back to your goals and think about whether you have gotten where you wanted to go or whether changes to procedures or updates to goals are needed. Only by **combining and integrating all the pillars** in a planned way (taking care these projects are aligned) will **synergy occur**, and you will have a great chance of fully achieving all the **ultimate benefits — a healthy, wealthy, and happy retirement**.

Maybe you are scared about having to give up your favorite foods, starting exercise even though you haven't done anything for a long time, trying to be among people, or trying mindfulness. I know that overcoming addictions (to junk food, sitting for long periods of time, etc.) can be challenging. Every change is a challenge, and changing long-standing habits takes effort and discipline. You can do it. Just get started. Gradually, you will feel the first effects. Then introduce at least one new habit a week. Skip or substitute action steps that don't work for you. Create a flexible project to suit your needs and situation.

You may ask: *What if I only select some pieces from this book that directly apply to me?*

I would rather combine all the knowledge gained in this book. You have already selected the pieces and goals that directly apply to you in each pillar. You already have a strategy and a set of goals that you will continuously meet. If you are disciplined, **you will be invincible**. Step out. Believe there are bridges there. Don't listen to your saboteurs. Keep momentum. **Consistency and momentum are the most important parts of everything** — finance, health, relationships, Third Act preparation. I have broken this big topic down for you in this book.

Others have done it, so you can do it, too. I'll keep my fingers crossed. And feel free to ask for help, a consultation, or more detailed discussion on any of the topics mentioned whenever you need it. I can also share what worked for me specifically in each chapter and what didn't fit into the book.

The quality of your retirement will depend on the quality of your choices and planning. You determine your happiness and well-being by making the right choices and not adopting the choices of society or others. Put more effort into adding novelty to your life. Constantly challenge yourself with new activities and new, different places. Meet new people. Explore new things and new points of view. (31) **This project is yours.**

Belief is the most powerful thing. If you believe that you will have a great Third Act, you will see that everything you have done up to this point has a reason, and you are pulling it together. You have planned for the Third Act. Follow your plan and everything will come together. You are going to have a much better Third Act because you chose to, better than you may have believed before reading this book.

You have created the plan. Now go and execute it.

☐ **Homework**: Invest in a mentor or guide who has traveled the path before you. I can be your guide.

Thank you for reading this book.

Did you get all your questions answered? If not, or if there's anything you'd like to ask, I'm here to help.

Chapter 12: Beyond Pension, Social Security Administration, and 401(k)

Are you someone in the corporate world who is mid to late age, say, about 45 years old, maybe an executive, senior manager, or business owner? Not quite in your prime, but you can see that there is a time not too far away that you are going to be planning your retirement? The decades of your Third Act are not that far anymore. You start to realize you need to plan if you want to achieve everything that is possible for you to retire well and have your retirement years to be the best time of your life.

Do not count on your company or state to supply you with everything that you need to know or do for your retirement. And I mean not only the financials; there are four pillars that we have to prepare.

Have you ever asked yourself, *Why am I working so hard, maybe at the expense of my health? What other life aspects am I sacrificing? For how long will I want to go this way? What then?*

You may think: *I have my 401(k) (or other pension scheme). They're managing my funds. It's doing fine. I don't really need to think of anything else.* Yes, it's a great foundation but, generally, not great enough because of the risk of under-investment. The average 401(k) only survives 6-8 years in retirement, i.e., running out of money in less than 10 years. (158)

But there is more to that, as we talked about in other chapters. What you don't realize is what you don't know.

Think about what you're used to as an executive. Think of all the perks, like traveling without worrying about where the money's coming from (although I know traveling on business is different than on vacation). Unless you plan carefully, less income will be coming in in your Third Act, and you will have to manage this money differently. The mindset is different. But it's only one part.

Besides money, a job gives you some level of predictability, control, and social contact. Generally, you also get a sense of power, status, achievement, meaning, and, most important, purpose. All these other parts will change when your life changes.

For your social part, you need to learn to build a social network outside of the workplace.

And you need to think about exercise like your life depends on it, because it does.

You have to start thinking now that your diet needs to adjust to your age and health, because your digestive system is already different. All the previous dietary mistakes may already be taking their toll now. You may be lacking some necessary minerals in your body that you need to add and supplement.

You need to also look at what purpose you're going to have when you're no longer given a purpose from your work, something that will really match what is important to you.

Think about what "pillar" in your life has not been considered or given thought. Whatever just popped into mind is the area you need to focus on right now. Don't delay. What is important but not urgent eventually becomes urgent when left until later. Relook at that pillar again in this book and give yourself the gift of foresight. And maybe, just maybe, your Third Act will be the best part of your life after all.

William Jennings Bryan: "Destiny is not a matter of chance; it is a matter of choice. It is not a thing to be waited for; it is a thing to be achieved."

Last Thought

I know I shared a lot of stuff with you. I'm passionate about helping you have the best Third Act that you can possibly have. If there's one thing I can recommend, it's to take one step at a time. The journey of a thousand miles begins with the first step, so take the one that's easiest for you, or most important to you, or that will have the biggest impact in comparison to the effort needed, and do it.

If, for instance, it is your health, go back to the health section and start taking action.

If it's your finances, do the same thing. Look at what is more important to you, but then eventually get to all of them.

References/ Links to Books, Websites, and Other Resources

(1) Susan Pinker: https://www.ted.com/playlists/620/what_s_the_secret_to_living_longer

(2) Marshall Goldsmith   https://www.marshallgoldsmith.com/

(3) Příjemný zralý věk (several authors; in Czech) https://www.databazeknih.cz/knihy/prijemny-zraly-vek-422369
Several articles of J. Hrstková in Hospodářské Noviny, …   (in Czech)

(4) Cyril Höschl: interview on radio Leonardo Plus 5. 11. 2017 (in Czech)

(5) Dan Ariely: https://www.ted.com/talks/dan_ariely_are_we_in_control_of_our_own_decisions#t-1006498

(6) https://archiv.ihned.cz/c1-66864660-jak-se-letos-nezblaznit-z-pandemie-projevujte-vdek-a-naucte-se-zasnout (in Czech)

(7) *The Good Gut* – Justin and Erica Sonnenburg

(8) Prof. Kolář – *Life In Motion: The Power of Physical Therapy*

(9) Gundry: *The Plant Paradox*

(10) Dotlich, Noel, & Walker, 2004: Critical learning experiences for leaders

(11) Chudlíková, Ludwig https://www.youtube.com/watch?v=-33-Fqothjl   (in Czech)

(12) https://hbr.org/2021/01/this-two-minute-morning-practice-will-make-your-day-better?ab=hero-main-text

(13) A lot of people don't want to see that they need change. Often it's only a crisis that forces them to change, but by then it's too late, says the coach https://domaci.ihned.cz/c7-66870870-1-16ed2341d62ef63 (in Czech)

(14) Feel-Good Happiness vs. Value-Based Happiness, https://vshapefit.wordpress.com/2013/04/07/443/

(15) Breathing correctly: https://www.redbull.com/cz-cs/videos/podcast-tema-dana-trzila-video-dychani (in Czech)

(16) Brian Tracy: 12 Step Goal-Setting Guide

(17) Hrstková: The unknown life of Czech pensioners: how much money do they need? Official statistics know almost nothing https://archiv.ihned.cz/c1-66730490-neznamy-zivot-ceskych-duchodcu-kolik-penez-potrebuji-oficialni-statistiky-nevedi-skoro-nic (in Czech)

(18) Respekt 8.2.2021, str. 45 (in Czech)

(19) Brian Tracy: No Excuses

(20) Shirzad Chamine: *Positive Intelligence* (course and a book)

(21) Vollmer: Gesunder darm, gesundes leben

(22) Collen: *10% Human: How Your Body's Microbes Hold the Key to Health and Happiness*

(23) Brian Tracy: Daily Habits of Successful People https://www.youtube.com/watch?v=nu5I85_Yaak

(24) Don't want to retire? Here's how to maintain a fulfilling career into your 80s and beyond https://www.washingtonpost.com/lifestyle/wellness/older-worker-career-success-habit/2021/03/01/f2803642-7787-11eb-948d-19472e683521_story.html

(25) Petr Kain v Hospodářské noviny https://archiv.ihned.cz/c1-66895830-pandemie-jako-kolektivni-trauma-nasledky-mohou-nest-jeste-deti-nasich-nenarozenych-deti (in Czech)

(26) Kerry Patterson, Joseph Grenny, Ron McMillan, Al Switzler: *Crucial Conversations: Tools for Talking When Stakes Are High*

(27) Rethinking Success https://www.getabstract.com/en/summary/rethinking-success/39655?_hsmi=117487035&_hsenc=p2Anqtz-_62ZZxMAS4MqHLoTNkFg4Ve6V1geri7a6ll-heWujPZFISyRIJP03cQg06MoDWZwo73IgLeqn1boTsKec-CISgIMYws7Rw

(28) Matthew Walker: *Why We Sleep: Unlocking the Power of Sleep and Dreams*

(29) Extreme Ownership Jocko Willink, https://www.youtube.com/watch?v=Ijqra3BcqWM

(30) https://www.novinky.cz/zena/styl/clanek/kdy-byva-ji-lide-nejstastnejsi-40357793#dop_ab_variant=0&dop_source_zone_name=novinky.sznhp.box&dop_req_id=ndxpLjen-QyR-20210430124&dop_id=40357793&source=hp&seq_no=6 (in Czech); https://www.theatlantic.com/health/archive/2014/11/where-age-equals-happiness/382434/ (in Czech)

(31) Ernie J. Zelinski: *How to Retire Happy, Wild, and Free*

(32) Cal Newport: *So Good They Can't Ignore You*

(33) Bill Perkins: *Die With Zero* (2020)

(34) https://www.pantheralife.co.uk/

(35) Report by Aegon (https://www.aegon.co.uk/advisers/advice-makes-sense/retirement-advice-in-the-uk-report.html) and Next Wealth (https://www.ftadviser.com/retirement-income/2021/08/20/four-in-five-advisers-ask-retirement-clients-about-happiness/?page=1)

(36) Marisa Murgatroyd, Live Your Message live, 2022

(37) Alex Korb: *The Upward Spiral* (https://www.getabstract.com/en/summary/the-upward-spiral/37422?_hsmi=208320210&_hsenc=p2Anqtz-9LoclTWA8VHm_8E8qZ-S2E7ivHNjUiOgvr4r5DASfxbl2T0_TnYrhmcm18Gxo2S8dJox-7Tnyv7lj3MZFKlhbhM7EhPa5A)

(38) Je možné si koupit štěstí? Uspokojení s pomocí peněz je možné. Za dodržení čtyř pravidel https://vikend.hn.cz/c1-67058100-je-mozne-si-koupit-stesti-dosahnout-uspokojeni-s-pomoci-penez-je-mozne-za-dodrzeni-ctyr-pravidel (in Czech)

(39) Masterclass Ocean and John Robbins: https://thriving.foodrevolution.org/masterclass/watch/?registrationId=7056f762-1ffd-43fd-8724-4e245a2a1e99

(40) https://knowledge.wharton.upenn.edu/faculty/olivia-mitchell/ , How Prepared Are Americans for Retirement? : https://knowledge.wharton.upenn.edu/article/how-prepared-are-americans-for-retirement/?_hsmi=216619528&_hsenc=p2Anqtz-uROuG8nrsARmsUI3uBU7JMLiKO0GBcTlRh-3bezGD63d1Y0g3S6TT0d_lvP8sYplud23wO6fjW3I31yaCfqg-Dr7UtTkQ

(41) Sönke Ahrens: *How to Take Smart Notes: One Simple Technique to Boost Writing, Learning and Thinking*

(42) https://inflammationseries.com/

(43) https://longevity.stanford.edu/wp-content/up-loads/2022/04/Short-Report-2.pdf

(44) Environmental Working Group annual summary "Dirty Dozen and Clear 15", e.g. here: https://edition.cnn.com/2022/04/07/health/dirty-dozen-produce-2022-wellness/index.html, https://s3.documentcloud.org/documents/21579810/dirty-dozen-and-clean-fifteen.pdf

(45) Modern Midlife Mentors

(46) https://theartofantiaging.com/top-causes-of-feeling-tired-all-the-time/

(47) Nathan Crane https://event.webinarjam.com/live/19/78xnla3t4ztk69bz96g

(48) Columbus Batiste in https://www.foodrev-olutionsummit.org/replays-2de/?j=132766&sfmc_sub-=61417587&l=137_HTML&u=1620823&mid=514008241&-jb=13014

(49) Julie Beck, The Atlantic Media Co., in Respekt 27.6.2022 (in Czech)

(50) Daniel Gladiš in: https://hn.cz/site/api/provide/yhmvB0NjD5Ee6WtgA4pHTMu9lGoPOUqc/77554290/Special_HN_Rentier.pdf (in Czech)

(51) Dr. Joel Fuhrman M.D. and Jonathan Hunsaker in https://supplementsrevealed.com/e2-dse/ and https://supplementsrevealed.com/replay-gsu/

(52) Richard Leider – What Do You Want to Be When You Grow Old? The Path of Purposeful Aging, in https://www.youtube.com/watch?v=s-LNO3Bdlwg

(53) Dr. Edward F. Group III in https://supplementsrevealed.com/e4-jdz/

(54) Julie Hrstková in HN 7.7.2022 p. 13 (in Czech)

(55) https://healthglade.com/ultimate-holistic-health-summit-latest-breakthroughs-you-havent-heard-of/?vgo_ee=xsLUcJFuQKNjOpZrAnnlUialM8cYVH5YoxCPei5gz%-2Fo%3D

(56) https://time.com/3929990/americans-over-weight-obese/

(57) Nathan Crane, President, Panacea Community, LLC, Director, Health and Healing Club, Host, Conquering Cancer Summit (email 23.7.2022)

(58) The New Map of Life, The Stanford Center of Longevity, https://longevity.stanford.edu/wp-content/uploads/2022/04/Short-Report-2.pdf

(59) Nathan Crane: *Becoming Cancer Free* https://www.dropbox.com/s/cf6qejaana8x4e5/Becoming%20Cancer-Free%20Manuscript.pdf?dl=0

(60) How much money would you need to live your ideal life? https://qz.com/2185504/how-much-money-would-you-need-to-live-your-ideal-life/

(61) How much money do people need to be happy? https://qz.com/1211957/how-much-money-do-people-need-to-be-happy/

(62) T. Harv Eker: *Secrets of the Millionaire Mind*

(63) David G. Blanchflower: Is happiness U-shaped everywhere? https://www.nber.org/system/files/working_papers/w26641/w26641.pdf

(64) JJ Virgin: *The Ultimate Health Roadmap*, https://whattoeat.byhealthmeans.com/reg-thank-you/#free-gifts

(65) This 75-Year Harvard Study Found the 1 Secret to Leading a Fulfilling Life. Here's some wisdom gleaned from one of the longest longitudinal studies ever conducted. https://www.inc.com/melanie-curtin/want-a-life-of-fulfillment-a-75-year-harvard-study-says-to-prioritize-this-one-t.html

(66) https://themakingofamillionaire.com/use-these-6-unsexy-money-lessons-to-become-a-multi-millionaire-e9db5698d9d6

(67) Tomáš Sedláček: Jak nebýt blb. Aneb ekonomické evangelium ke konci prázdnin, https://archiv.hn.cz/c1-67106980-jak-nebyt-blb-aneb-ekonomicke-evangelium-ke-konci-prazdnin (in Czech)

(68) Purpose And Power In Retirement : New Opportunities for Meaning and Significance, https://www.semanticscholar.org/paper/Purpose-And-Power-In-Retirement-%3A-New-Opportunities-Koenig/68f5da46f6917d02b-29c83089029e98e91309a5d

(69) Respekt 31/2022 (in Czech)

(70) Lubna Samara: "Values: How They Can Work For You" (https://www.higherwill.co.uk/hw-blog/values)

(71) Darius Foroux: "4 Toxic Money Beliefs That Keep You From Financial Freedom," https://dariusforoux.medium.com/4-toxic-money-beliefs-that-keep-you-from-financial-freedom-1266097a4d45

(72) https://archiv.hn.cz/c1-67110020-sazet-na-zvestovatele-akciovych-krachu-co-se-obcas-trefi-rozumny-investor-udela-jinou-vec   (in Czech)

(73) Peter Ludwig: *The End of Procrastination*

(74) James Clear: *The Power of Small Steps*

(75) Andy Storch: *Own Your Career, Own Your Life*, https://www.getabstract.com/en/summary/own-your-career-own-your-life/41153?af=getContext&_hsmi=225872001

(76) Darshak Rana: 7 Mindless Money Wasters People Think Are Acceptable, https://medium.com/mind-l/7-mindless-money-wasters-people-think-are-acceptable-7b56f7353499

(77) Does Market Timing Work? https://www.schwab.com/learn/story/does-market-timing-work

(78)   https://www.pantheralife.co.uk/retirement-survey-panthera-life/

(79) More than half of over-40s feel anxious about retiring, survey suggests, https://www.independent.co.uk/money/retirement-anxiety-finances-savings-b2146178.html

(80) Alex Mathers: 7 'superficial' tips that will get you 10X further in life, https://iamalexmathers.medium.com/7-superficial-tips-that-will-get-you-10x-further-in-life-82a9b19b2961

(81) Robert Roy Britt: Arthritis Cases Skyrocket as ⯑1 Remedy is Often Ignored, https://robertroybritt.medium.com/arthritis-cases-skyrocket-as-1-remedy-is-often-ignored-4adc119fdf83

(82) Gary Foster: How to Avoid Becoming a "Bored Boomer", https://www.linkedin.com/pulse/how-avoid-becoming-bored-boomer-part-one-foster-ncrw-ncope-cprc/?trackingId=iQjcmH8QQkKS3OR3AuNqlg%3D%3D, https://www.linkedin.com/pulse/how-avoid-becoming-bored-boomer-part-two-foster-ncrw-ncope-cprc/, https://www.linkedin.com/pulse/how-avoid-becoming-bored-boomer-part-three-foster-ncrw-ncope-cprc/?trackingId=CMGi-FyEkRa6TkHwjF2FIYg%3D%3D

(83) Tim Denning, You Don't Lack Talent. You Lack Consistency: https://medium.com/mlclyou-dont-lack-talent-you-lack-consistency-6c4f3bf5f195

(84) https://www.businesswire.com/news/home/20220824005247/en/New-Survey-Suggests-Americans-are-Worried-about-Outliving-Savings-While-Advisors-are-Confident-They-Can-Address-Client-Concerns?_hsmi=226498858

(85) Dan Buettner, Power 9: https://www.bluezones.com/2016/11/power-9/#

(86) The Four Pillars of the New Retirement: What a Difference a Year Makes, Investments & Wealth Institute, https://fs.hubspotusercontent00.net/hubfs/4812204/Insider%20Articles/2022/April%2011/IWM22JanFeb_TheFourPillarsoftheNewRetirement.pdf?_hsmi=230439539

(87) Leaky Gut Report: https://gutbrainseries.com/free-report/?a=5d8a8eec08401&b=bdfcc24f

(88) Achieve your full-life potential. Five Easy Steps to Living Longer, Healthier, and with more Purpose: https://makeagingwork.com/wp-content/uploads/2017/12/Achieve_Your_FULL_Potential-2-1.pdf

(89) Sandrine Thuret, You can grow new brain'cells. Here's how: https://www.ted.com/talks/sandrine_thuret_you_can_grow_new_brain_cells_here_s_how?subtitle=en

(90) Kdy se rodí přátelství, Respekt 42/2022: https://www.respekt.cz/tydenik/2022/42/kdy-se-rodi-pratelstvi?issueId=100589 (in Czech)

(91) Dr. Fuhrman, MD, https://shop.supplementsrevealed.com/se-masterclass-launch/

(92) sleepassociation.org 2015: sleep-journal.com 2017, in https://edu.redbuttonedu.cz/neuroplasticita-aneb-dalnice-v-mozku/ (in Czech)

(93) Dr Jokers: Best Intermittent Fasting Strategies & How to Fast: https://drjockers.com/best-intermittent-fasting-strategies/

(94) Dr Jokers: Top 12 Immune Support Strategies to Thrive in Life: https://drjockers.com/immune-support-strategies/

(95) Norman P. Li, S. Kanazawa: Country roads, take me home... to my friends: How intelligence, population density, and friendship affect modern happiness. British journal of psychology. https://elicit.org/search?q=How+does+the+number+of+friends+someone+has+affect+their+overall+happiness%3F&token=01GH6QNE661AJRF0TZHAAA5C8Z&paper=1c2cdd3b-d387af8fa2cd73e9e00561bdc025f8a5&column=title

W. Bruine de Bruin, Andrew M. Parker, J. Strough: Age differences in reported social networks and well-being. Psychology and aging. https://elicit.org/search?q=How+does+the+number+of+friends+someone+has+affect+their+overall+happiness%3F&token=01GH6QNE661AJRF0TZHAAA5C8Z&paper=5533b701f80d4c0b8e77142afd86468421e969d3&column=takeaway

(96) Alex Mathers : https://static1.squarespace.com/static/5dee42c4ad5fad5d9c6510bb/t/623ee95dfc3b0e1fd-2c1abaf/1648290149051/12HabitsMentallyStrong.pdf

(97) Daně a penzijní systém. Česko si z „úkolů" zesnulého nobelisty Prescotta vybralo lehčí půlku: https://archiv.hn.cz/c1-67134910-dane-a-penzijni-system-cesko-si-z-bdquo-ukolu-ldquo-zesnuleho-nobelisty-prescotta-vybralo-lehci-pulku (in Czech)

(98) Work forever: Japan's seniors brace for life without retirement, https://www.japantimes.co.jp/news/2022/10/17/business/senior-employment-japan/, and https://www.e15.cz/zahranicni/prace-navzdy-japonsti-seniori-se-pripravu-ji-na-zivot-bez-odchodu-do-duchodu-1394138 (in Czech)

(99) Brian Tracy: *Reinvention - How to Make the Rest of Your Life the Best of Your Life*

(100) Sanjay Gupta: *Keep Sharp: Build a Better Brain at Any Age*

(101) https://storypowermarketing.com/wp-content/uploads/2021/09/5-Storytelling-Secrets-from-Story-Power-Marketing-v2.2.pdf

(102) World's Retirees Risk Running Out of Money a Decade Before Death, https://www.bloomberg.com/news/articles/2019-06-13/world-s-retirees-risk-running-out-of-money-a-decade-before-death

(103) You have ample savings. So why are you scared of running out of money?, https://www.marketwatch.com/story/you-have-ample-savings-so-why-are-you-scared-of-running-out-of-money-2020-09-29

(104) If Career Defined You, How Do You Find Fulfillment in Retirement?, https://makeagingwork.com/2022/10/18/if-career-defined-you-how-do-you-find-fulfillment-in-retirement/

(105) Here's What a $2 Million Retirement Looks Like in America, https://www.wsj.com/articles/heres-what-a-2-million-retirement-looks-like-in-america-11661702455

(106) https://procne.hn.cz/c1-67105550-zit-bez-planu-tomas-berdych-po-kariere-sbira-zazitky-dal-se-na-golf-a-zase-hraje-tenis (in Czech)

(107) https://cruciallearning.com/blog/helping-your-adult-child-build-better-habits/

(108) https://archiv.hn.cz/c1-67109780-game-set-rodina-odchazi-jedna-z-nejvetsich-sportovkyn-historie-serena-williamsova (in Czech)

(109) Mindful Self-Discipline, https://www.getabstract.com/en/summary/mindful-self-discipline/44850?af=getContext&_hsmi=227424060

(110) Tim Denning, Eighteen (Short) Reasons Most People Aren't Millionaires: https://medium.com/swlh/eighteen-short-reasons-most-people-arent-millionaires-1ed-0bc436688

(111) https://dariusforoux.medium.com/what-would-you-do-if-you-were-rich-8e5b11947eda

(112) The 2022 Food Revolution Summit, https://www.foodrevolutionsummit.org/replays-2de/?j=132766&sfmc_sub=61417587&l=137_HTML&u=1620823&mid=514008241&jb=13014

(113) What's the Deal with Carbs?, https://goodnesslover.com/blogs/health/what-s-the-deal-with-carbs/?

(114) Autoimmune Diet: Top 12 Best Foods to Reduce Inflammation, https://drjockers.com/autoimmune-diet/

(115) Top Longevity Supplements to Take for Anti-Aging, https://drjockers.com/longevity-supplements/?ck_subscriber_id=1777918713

(116) Strong K., Mathers C., Leeder S., Beaglehole R. Preventing chronic diseases: how many lives can we save? Lancet. 2005; 366: 1578-1582

(117) Take Control of Your Brain's Destiny, https://scienceofprevention.com/

(118) Plant-Based Protein: The Best Sources & How Much You Actually Need, https://foodrevolution.org/blog/plant-based-protein/?j=149571&sfmc_sub=61417587&l=137_HTML&u=1871160&mid=514008241&jb=1109

(119) Carbohydrate quality and human health: a series of systematic reviews and meta-analyses, https://www.thelancet.com/journals/lancet/article/PIIS0140-6736(18)31809-9/fulltext

(120) "No More Sugar Cravings?", https://shop.eattolivemasterclass.com/sugar-detox-masterclass?vgo_ee=UjRA4y%2FfP3Bxbio71KuIxCaIM8cYVH5YOxCPei5gz%2Fo%3D

(121) Healthy Heart, Module #2: Eat Well for Your Heart, https://community.foodrevolution.org/products/hhc/eat-well-for-your-heart/

(122) https://www.redbuttonedu.cz/wp-content/uploads/2022/08/BrainBreakfast-18.8.2022-Vlado-Zlatos-Zdravi.pdf (in Czech)

(123) Detoxify Your Body with InfraRed Sauna, https://drjockers.com/infrared-sauna/

(124) 15 Zinc Deficiency Symptoms and Best Food Sources, https://drjockers.com/15-zinc-deficiency-symptoms/?ck_subscriber_id=1777918713; http://www.who.int/publications/cra/chapters/volume1/0257-0280.pdf

(125) Ocean Robbins: Why You May Want to Choose a Plant-Based Diet for Hypertension + 9 Best Foods for Blood Pressure, https://foodrevolution.org/blog/foods-for-blood-pressure/?j=170428&sfmc_sub=61417587&l=137_HTML&u=2209057&mid=514008241&jb=130

(126) https://designretirement.org/contact/

(127) Darshak Rana, 11 Life Cheat Codes I've Proudly Stolen From People Smarter Than Me: https://medium.com/awesomehumans/11-things-ive-proudly-stolen-from-people-smarter-than-me-d088b9d39a65

(128) Jussi Luukkonen, Do 50+ Men Have A Future?: https://medium.com/illumination/do-50-men-have-a-future-ab2ff6b303c6

(129) Top 12 Best Magnesium Rich Foods, https://drjockers.com/best-magnesium-rich-foods/

(130) Global Council on Brain Health (GCBH), Brain Food: GCBH Recommendations on Nourishing Your Brain Health; https://en.uoa.gr/fileadmin/user_upload/PDF-files/anakoinwseis/genikes_anakoinwseis/2018/070218_brain_food.pdf

(131) Shawn Achor, TEDx Bloomington: https://www.ted.com/talks/shawn_achor_the_happy_secret_to_better_work

(132) The Ant And The Grasshopper Story With Moral, https://www.lifelords.com/story/ant-and-the-grasshopper-story/

(133) 1 in 8 Americans over 50 show signs of food addiction, U-M poll finds, https://www.eurekalert.org/news-releases/977872?_kx=clz02SAYvYwdeCYBm6is0fa1_B9GIOegD-IXjZ69vFw%3D.Syeesf

(134) Svačiny jsou přežitek, tři jídla denně stačí, říkají experti, https://archiv.hn.cz/c1-67163720-svaciny-jsou-prezitek-tri-jidla-denne-staci-rikaji-experti (in Czech)

(135) https://archiv.hn.cz/c1-67168890-kila-ubudou-portfolio-nabobtna-investori-sonduji-potencial-novych-leku-na-hubnuti (in Czech)

(136) Bronnie Ware: Top Five Regrets of the Dying: A Life Transformed by the Dearly Departing

(137) Ageing Europe - statistics on pensions, income and expenditure, https://ec.europa.eu/eurostat/statistics-explained/index.php?title=Ageing_Europe_-_statistics_on_pensions,_income_and_expenditure

(138) Wes Moss: You Can Retire Sooner Than You Think, You Can Retire Sooner Than You Think

(139) James Clear: Atomic Habits

(140) Barry Miles: Many Years from Now , https://www.goodreads.com/book/show/305955.Paul_McCartney

(141) Malcolm Gladwell: Outliers, https://www.amazon.com/Outliers-Story-Success-Malcolm-Gladwell/dp/0316017930

(142) The 4% rule — FIRE calculation (aka Financial Independence/Retire Early), https://www.mustachianpost.com/2020/05/31/how-to-calculate-early-retirement-fire-aka-financial-independence/

(143) https://elicit.org/search?q=How+much+does+retirement+satisfaction+increase+with+assets%3F&token=01GW7SNJ71BDVXFFRJH8AHYQH5

(144) Elizabeth Blackburn on the telomere effect: 'It's about keeping healthier for longer', https://www.theguardian.com/science/2017/jan/29/telomere-effect-elizabeth-blackburn-nobel-prize-medicine-chromosomes

(145) https://www.who.int

(146) MoSCoW method, https://en.wikipedia.org/wiki/MoSCoW_method

(147) Martin Seligman and the Rise of Positive Psychology, https://www.neh.gov/article/martin-seligman-and-rise-positive-psychology

(148) An 85-year Harvard study found the No. 1 thing that makes us happy in life: It helps us 'live longer', https://www.cnbc.com/2023/02/10/85-year-harvard-study-found-the-secret-to-a-long-happy-and-successful-life.html

(149) New Report Finds Links Between 'Mental Well-Being' and Brain Health, https://www.aarp.org/health/brain-health/info-2018/mental-well-being-connection-report.html

(150) James Clear: How Long Does it Actually Take to Form a New Habit?, https://jamesclear.com/new-habit

(151) Prescription for living longer: Spend less time alone, https://news.byu.edu/news/prescription-living-longer-spend-less-time-alone

(152) A smartphone app reveals erratic diurnal eating patterns in humans that can be modulated for health benefits, https://www.ncbi.nlm.nih.gov/pmc/articles/PMC4635036/ , as discussed in Energy Blueprint Masterclass, https://theenergyblueprint.com/new-science-of-energy1/?inf_contact_key=98e978c9742c548d59fd52eca676505acb2dfb2519c-88201cb0488cbdb276db5

(153) Graham Lawton: This Book Could Save Your Life, 2020

(154) my conversation with Jim Connolly

(155) Global AgeWatch Index 2015: Insight report, summary and methodology, http://www.globalagewatch.org/reports/global-agewatch-index-2015-insight-report-summary-and-methodology/

(156) Peter Attia, MD: Outlive

(157) Ahlskog, J. E., Geda, Y. E., Graff-Radford, N. R., & Petersen, R. C. (2011). Physical exercise as a preventive or disease-modifying treatment of dementia and brain aging. Mayo Clinic Proceedings, 86(9), 876-884.

(158) Begin with Retirement in Mind - Your Retirement Goals, https://retirehappy.thinkific.com/courses/take/retire-happy-planning-course/lessons/43730707-begin-with-retirement-in-mind-your-retirement-goals

(159) Dr. Tal Ben-Shahar: https://event.webinarjam.com/live/68/27q6mtlou36bg2p52up72qm

(160) Thomas Stanley & William Danko: The Millionaire Next Door

(161) The Many Faces of Retirement with Dorian Mintzer and Dr. George Schofield, https://www.buzzsprout.com/1881506/12899319-the-many-faces-of-retirement-with-dorian-mintzer-and-dr-george-schofield

(162) https://archiv.hn.cz/c1-67225000-za-rok-a-pul-muze-mit-demenci-v-cesku-200-tisic-lidi-je-nekolik-zpusobu-jak-vlohy-k-nemoci-zvratit (in Czech)

Templates, Checklists, Tools, Color legend

To download the free Templates, Checklists, Tools, Color legend, to work with this book, that are mentioned in some chapters, visit **www.livingyourbestthirdact.com**, or for your convenience, scan the QR code below.

www.livingyourbestthirdact.com

Milan Schwarzkopf received his MSc and PhD from the Czech Technical University and MBA from Rochester Institute of Technology. Milan is also an accredited coach. He spent his working years as an (Interim) Senior Project and Program Manager on large scale, strategic, multimillion, complex, critical global projects (banks, telco operators, system integrators), managing large and global distributed/virtual multi-expert teams (EU, Asia, US). He also established three startups. Milan is known for living the Third Act experiences he writes about.

Like most responsible people, he had created a healthy financial nest egg to take him through his own retirement. And like most people, doing a fair amount of travel and treating his last third of his life like an extended vacation, he soon learned the secret to having an exciting and meaningful retirement being more than just financial security.

Milan now lives in Prague, the Czech Republic. He likes skiing (both downhill and cross-country), riding his bike, mountaineering, and traveling all over the world, and he also used to practice rafting, kayaking, and rock climbing.

Speaking, Workshops, Online Courses and Coaching

If you'd like Milan to speak live or virtually at your next event, conference, or meeting, please reach us by visiting our web site, www.thirdactresources.com or for your convenience, scan the QR code below.

Also, Milan is available for the following:

- — Live & Virtual Workshops
- — Podcasts
- — Radio
- — Television
- — Breakout Sessions
- — Keynote

Once again, visit our web site, www.thirdactresources.com or for your convenience, scan the QR code below.

www.thirdactresources.com

Made in United States
North Haven, CT
10 January 2025

64250876R00150